Praise for It's All Narrative

"I am honoured to have worked with supporting and changing the lives of others.

"I absolutely love this book; it has an abundance of practical, useful and, most importantly, meaningful 'take aways', resulting in the ideas being much more likely to be put into practice.

"Nick can be proud of all he has done to help others in order to have the wisdom and knowledge to write the excellent content."

Helen Morton (parent and head teacher of All Saints Primary School)

"A beautiful book. I have certainly been left wanting more and wishing I had known this stuff earlier in my life—both as a parent and a professional."

Eleanor Losse (parent, step-parent and head teacher of
Manchester Grammar Junior School)

"I have always liked that Nick's work is based in practical terms—what to say or do. It is not just a theoretical approach, and this comes across strongly in this short, readable and easily accessible book.

"Reading *It's all Narrative* has given me a renewed sense of vigour, and I will be using Transformative Communication at the forefront of my teaching/leadership styles."

Tracy Kendrick (head teacher of Hursthead Junior School)

"Such an easy read, but with such insightful advice.

"I know it's good, because I often find it an effort to read work-related things but honestly just wanted to keep reading!

"I will be recommending it to all of our staff when it is published."

Claire Love (parent and head teacher of Lane End Primary School)

"Nick has written a book that is supportive and full of strategies that can easily be tried and taken on board.

"The way Nick writes is easy to read, and this would be a helpful resource for any parent.

"Through opening up and sharing his own challenges, Nick allows the reader to feel a shared understanding that the challenges we meet with our children are quite normal and more common than we may think.

"The number of case studies allow us an insight into the strategies in practice and how, although they are not going to be easy, if you persevere, you will be successful.

"Nick has shown fantastic perseverance in overcoming challenges and should be proud of his achievements and the compassion he so eloquently writes with throughout this book."

Vicky Walker (parent and head teacher of Ludworth Primary School)

It's All Narrative

It's All Narrative

How to Build Resilience in Children Through the Use of Transformative Communication

NICK DUX

THE CHOIR PRESS

First published in the United Kingdom in 2022 by
The Choir Press

ISBN 978-1-78963-262-0

Contents

In loving memory of Milly Townley, a truly Transformative teacher and a wonderful person who is missed by all who had the pleasure of knowing her.

Acknowledgements

In the spirit of the 'attitude of gratitude' that I reference later in the book, I have many people I would like to acknowledge in helping me—wittingly or not—in coming to the point of writing this book:

Firstly, thank you, Mum, for bringing me into the world, loving me and caring for me.

Thank you, Dad, for teaching me that relentlessness, determination and drive will get me much further than feeling sorry for myself. Thank you for your pride in me and for providing me with great opportunities in life.

Thank you to my beautiful wife, Erin, for taking the children out on those rainy days when I said I needed to work on 'My Book'. Thank you for being my soundboard, for having a quiet confidence in me and for calming me down when I started to worry. I love you.

Thank you to my lovely sisters: Paula—my second mum and provider of so many happy memories when I was growing up—you cared for, loved and nurtured me, and I will never forget that; and Julie—my antagonist turned best friend!—you have a great way of helping me see a different perspective, a wonderful sense of humour that always makes me laugh and you also gave me opportunities to learn Resilience from a very young age! Thank you both.

Thank you to my friend and 'motivation buddy', Richard Cundiff. Without you and your assertion—"You could write a book, Duxy. No problem!"—this book would not exist. Your time, support and insight are so much appreciated.

Thank you to Jim Nicholson, head teacher of Mellor Primary School—the only head teacher who, when I was a young naive family resource worker, showed me around his school and introduced me to every member of his staff. Your continued time and guidance have been priceless.

Acknowledgements

Thank you, Eleanor Losse. I have always felt valued in your school and in your company and appreciate your unwavering support.

Thank you, Matt Carroll, Vicky Walker, Ed Milner, Joanne Marrow, Claire Love, Alison White and Tracy Kendrick. Your trust in me has given me huge confidence to implement my approach within your schools, and that confidence has grown to help me achieve my goal of writing this book.

Thank you, Andy Buckler, Liz Irvin, Amanda Cornwall, Stephen Murphy, Christine Meekley, Michelle Smart and Helen Hilton for supporting the evolution of Transformative Communication and welcoming me into your schools.

Thank you to the other head teachers who have allowed me the privilege of working with their staff and children: Erica Reyes, Gill Holmes, Vicky MacPherson, Katherine Muncaster and Liz Mason. Special mention also to Gemma Parkin, Helen Peace and Gill Collins. Your support and positivity towards my approach has been unwavering, and that has not gone unnoticed.

Thank you to Richard Davis, my lecturer at UCLAN and one of the most inspiring people I have come across. I still quote you many times and think of you often. It was also you who put me in touch with Robin Bailey and the meta-cognitive therapy course that set the wheels in motion for me to make the positive changes that have led me to this point. I hope you now know you have had a huge impact on me.

Thank you to Andrew Holt, Janette Braithwaite, Gareth Edwards, Sarah Chatterton and Anna Purvis. You were with me when I was at my most inconsistent and gave me the opportunity to work through issues and become a much-improved version of myself than the one who stood before you. Gareth, your words and time when I was going through periods of anxiety led me to make decisions that had a positive and far-reaching impact on my life.

Thank you to the thousands of young people I have been honoured to work with in so many different schools over the years. Without you, this book has little content. Some of you have made me laugh, some have made me cry (tears of joy and sadness), but all of you have taught me something, so I write this book with all of you in mind.

Thank you to the people who do not know me, have never met me and yet have had such a positive impact on my life: Les Brown, Tony Robbins, Jack Canfield, Susan Jeffers, Louise Haye (RIP), Byron Katie, Dr Joe Dispenza, Rhonda Byrne, Michael Beckwith, Tom Bird and Jeremy Cassell, Viktor Frankl (RIP) and Marci Shimoff.

Thank you to all at The Choir Press for your time, advice and patience in the process of publishing "It's All Narrative". I am particularly grateful to David Onyett, Naomi Music, Rachel Woodman and Adrian Sysum for your support. I thought publishing my first book would be frought with stress, but you have alleviated much of that and you are greatly appreciated.

Finally, thank you to my four beautiful children who continue to teach me more than I teach them. You, to me, are everything.

I dedicate this book to the memory of Karen Marsden. We miss you every day. Your spirit and energy live with us, and you are our guardian angel.

Foreword

by Jim Nicholson

Having been in a senior position of school leadership since December 2001, with a wide range of ever-developing responsibilities, I eventually became the head teacher of Mellor Primary School, Stockport, in September 2007.

The world of teaching and leading a school was very different back in 2001. If children in our care demonstrated emotional problems, anger issues or difficulties in developing effective, compassionate relationships, the answer was to have children referred, so that someone employed through the local authority services for children could then talk to them about their problems—a sticky-plaster approach to deeper-routed issues.

It was through this that I first met the younger Nick Dux, who was just at the start of his developing career. While many aspects of working in a school have changed dramatically, there are some crucial aspects that have remained constant: it has remained essential to surround oneself with the best self-motivated, dedicated people in the job, in order for us to ensure that the resources available provide the best possible services and outcomes for our children and families. Nick Dux is such a professional. It has been a privilege to watch his personal growth during these years and how he has helped and supported our children and families across a period of exponential change. Nick has had the drive to find better ways to address the ever-changing issues that have presented themselves.

Technological, economic and social changes have impacted upon the young people we serve. Mental wellness and the need to focus on personal development have certainly become more prevalent due to these changes. The inner voice of our children is often the blocker for future success; it can be the inhibitor of potential, and yet this aspect has been a key feature missing in the training programme for professionals working with young people.

Professionals, parents and carers alike call out for greater understanding and approaches through which we can address personal development for the long-term future of our children.

In response, our school became the first recognised Positive Education School through our work with psychologist, Julie Hurst, following the PERMA model developed by the word-renowned Martin Seligman. We celebrated these successes, but more was needed; yet, where does one find such material? There is a plethora of books available on personal development, but within the sphere linking good education practice and parenting, there has been a void ...

Nick Dux's work now completes the jigsaw. Through his personal development, reflective practice, research and working with children and families over the last sixteen years, he has created a diet of language known as Transformative Communication, which provides a clear base for any professional, parent or carer. This approach builds the Resilience needed within our young people and has the gift of life-changing potential.

Through Nick's holistic and consistent Transformative Communication approach, we can now embark on an exciting journey that has the potential to transform our children's self-belief, change their inner voice, build Resilience and ultimately help us to understand their behaviour, impacting positively upon their potential for future success.

On reading this book, you will be empowered by the material and approaches that will make a difference to your young people, with the added bonus of understanding your own inner voice and how you may meet your own inhibitive behaviours. Be changed by using Transformative Communication.

Jim Nicholson, BA (Hons), PGCE, NPQH, Forest School L3

CHAPTER 1

It's All Narrative

A person's 'internal narrative' is the story they tell themselves about themselves and the world around them. We all have an internal narrative, whether we are aware of it or not. It includes things like the judgements we make without thinking about it, uninvestigated thoughts that we take to be definitely true, what we like and dislike, what we expect from our lives, and much more. You may hear someone saying, "Knowing my luck, it will rain" when they are going on a holiday; we may laugh and shrug, but this indicates that the person making the comment has an internal narrative that expects negative things to happen to them. The internal narrative is informed by the 'inner voice' which is built in a person's formative years from early experiences, messages received about themselves and their relationships and attachments with key people. A person with a negative internal narrative will often struggle to have sufficient Resilience to cope in challenging times; indeed, they may find negatives even when life is kind to them. Subsequently, the behaviour of a person is a direct translation of their inner voice. If the inner voice feeds a destructive internal narrative, Resilience is reduced, and this is reflected by behaviour.

Transformative Communication, an approach I have created and use in schools, refers to simple, specific and effective changes to communication that can:

TRANSFORM INTERNAL NARRATIVE ➡ TRANSFORM RESILIENCE ➡ TRANSFORM BEHAVIOUR

In the pages ahead I will illustrate how best to transform your child's internal narrative. It is this internal narrative that governs a child's levels of Resilience and, in turn, a child's behaviour.

Transformative Communication loosely comprises of two main strategies:

- *Superpower Language.* A proactive technique to empower your child's inner voice (internal narrative) and make them acutely aware of the strengths they have and how they use such strengths to positively impact on situations (whether they perceive that situation to be good, bad or indifferent).
- *Empathic and Empowering Language.* A specific reactive approach to behaviour (poor behaviour, anxiety, disproportionate responses to setbacks, sadness, emotional crisis and self-deprecating language). Empathic and Empowering language turns seemingly negative flashpoints into opportunities for growth, learning and positive Resilience.

Through applying the Transformative Communication approaches in this book, you can create a stronger internal narrative in your child(ren) that will help them to improve their Resilience, behaviour and relationships.

My name is Nick Dux. I am strong, I am committed, I am consistent, I am proactive and I am giving. A few years ago, writing these words about myself would have been followed by an uncomfortable wince! As a young boy I perceived messages implicitly and explicitly to form a story quite the opposite of that grand introduction. For many of the years that followed, I took those perceived messages to be true and subsequently lived in a small comfort zone for fear of the panic and anxiety attacks that frequented my days. Perhaps it is not a surprise that I have chosen to work in the field of children's mental health for the last sixteen years. My formative experiences have, however, allowed me to have a personal as well as professional passion for the well-being of children, and they have given me unique insight. I know how the child feels when they are 'misbehaving'. I also know the impact of the messages that adults give to a child as they grow—such messages stay lodged in the subconscious of children and grow into the firm beliefs they have about themselves. These limiting, and at times toxic, beliefs then infiltrate many areas of their adult life: their career, their relationships, their role as a parent and their happiness.

I also see things from the perspective of a parent. I now have four children who are wonderful and challenging in equal measure. I know first-hand that a child's behaviour can directly conflict with an adult's needs, and it is a huge ask of a parent to be positive during such times.

I have a degree in Human Communication and love going to the gym and watching my football team. Self-improvement is a daily discipline in my life; reading books, mindfulness, meditation, visualisation and affirmations have become an integral part of my story, making a huge impact on me, both personally and pro-fessionally.

For two years I have been self-employed, working in ten different schools to build Resilience through Transformative Communication as a whole-school approach. This has included leading education professionals in developing a style of specific communication that builds a strong internal narrative in children; changing the language towards poor behaviour; understanding why poor behaviour may be occurring; building staff Resilience and helping them see they have the tools to overcome the most challenging of situations; one-to-one work with parents; one-to-one work with children; and teaching whole classes about what Resilience means and the Superpowers children have that will help them achieve their potential.

Thankfully, my experiences, career, learning, studies and extensive self-improvement work have enabled me to develop some powerful tools to support parents in moving their child(ren) out of the negative cycle illustrated on page 4:

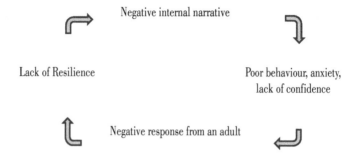

Negative internal narrative

Lack of Resilience

Poor behaviour, anxiety,
lack of confidence

Negative response from an adult

A child's perception is crucial within negative cycles, as their story leads to automatic negative perceptions that can become toxic beliefs that they have about themselves. I will discuss later how behaviour directly translates a child's toxic beliefs.

A child will never change without the key adults in their lives making some changes first. A child's responses are based on the view they have of themselves—something that is put there by adults and the world around them. Even seemingly premeditated and calculated behaviours come from a need that has not been met—usually a need that the child has from repeated experience of the cycle portrayed above. When an adult's responses are more consistently positive, their child will change without ever knowing they needed to in the first place. "All well and good, but how?" you may ask!

In this book I aim to provide you with specific Transformative Communication tools, and the reasons they work so well in improving your child's internal narrative/Resilience, and show the far-reaching impact this improvement can have. I also include real-life stories from my own experiences at the end of each chapter. Some of the ideas in this book will help you see a short-term benefit as your child's behaviour becomes more in line with what you expect, want and think you need. Furthermore, if the negative cycle illustrated above can be more consistently replaced by the more positive cycles I will detail in the pages ahead, your child could change their internal narrative and the way they view themselves to the point that they will use their beliefs about themselves to make better life decisions as they grow. So, for example, by taking on board the lessons in this book:

- If an older, 'cooler' kid were to offer alcohol or drugs at the park, your more Resilient child would like themselves enough to make an informed decision from a position of strength;
- If your child were to argue with their friends, they could know that they can solve the problem and be assertive and able to repair any damage done;
- If someone were to try to intimidate your child, they could carry themselves in a way that shows such assurance and strength, that the intimidator would look elsewhere;
- If your child were to realise a supposed friend was not actually a true friend, they could assertively but kindly walk away from that relationship with a grace of which you would be proud;
- If you had to speak sternly to your child, they wouldn't fall into an emotional crisis but could see how they acted, take responsibility for those actions and know they are able to move on.

All this equates to a sustainable change that would help your child become more Resilient and much more likely to navigate their way through life successfully (whatever success actually means to them). In other words, the consistent application of the approaches you will read about here can lead to a sustainable and positive change in your child's internal narrative and, with that, enhancement of their personal Resilience. Higher levels of Resilience lead to greater confidence, better choices, improved behaviour, healthier relationships, greater health, and happiness in the face of an ever-challenging world. Throughout this book I will refer to Resilience as being linked to a child's internal narrative; these two aspects of the way a child sees themselves go hand in hand, and the creation of a positive internal narrative (the goal of the book) will lead to a child having much greater Resilience. As well as looking at improvement of your child's Resilience, we will explore how to remove or overcome barriers you may encounter in trying to put the suggested strategies in place.

CHAPTER 2
How Do I Know?

You'll notice I begin the word 'Resilience' with a capital 'R' whether the word is at the start, middle or end of a sentence, just as religious scribes always start their chosen figure of divinity with a capital letter. Fear not; I won't muddy any waters by digressing into religion! But this illustrates the importance I place in Resilience. In recent years it has become a 'buzzword', though it is much more than that to me. Resilience underpins every person's ability to fulfil their potential. Lack of it belies a person's struggles and is often rooted in a poor internal narrative. We live in a world of labels—ADHD, ASD, PTSD, PDA, anxiety and depression to name but a few. Rarely do I ever come across a person with any of those conditions who, when I scratch beneath the surface, does not have a past that compromises their Resilience and their internal narrative. The irony in this is that most people are much more Resilient than they believe! Just look at what people have coped with during Covid times. So many stories of Resilience have emerged from people who completely surprised themselves; yet those same people will rarely value their achievements, an example of temporary and unrecognised Resilience.

Crucially, most people don't 'believe' in themselves. Their internal narrative hasn't changed, despite showing Resilience, so the people who coped so well during a global crisis will go back to questioning themselves when life settles down and there are, inevitably, new challenges to face.

I refer to the Resilience I encourage through Transformative Communication as 'positive Resilience'. "Surely all Resilience is positive?" I hear you ask. Not always. There are people who are extremely Resilient, but at some cost to themselves. That is, they go through a challenging time and come out of it relieved it is over and with a detrimental effect to their emotional, physical and/or mental health. I refer to this as 'survival Resilience'.

Positive Resilience refers to a person coming through a challenging situation knowing how they did it: what skills they used, what they learnt about themselves and how they can use this moving forward.

There is such a thing as 'false Resilience': someone who appears to be full of confidence, robust, strong and cocky—the person who tells anyone who will listen that they just "get on with it". Yet their behaviour in certain situations may tell a hugely different story. Perhaps they get angry easily, drink too much alcohol, take drugs and/or are unkind to the people closest to them—not the actions of a truly Resilient person with a strong internal narrative.

The seeds of the internal narrative begin as a young baby, picking up on people's body language and reading whether an adult is trustworthy or not. A young baby has an innate, almost primal instinct, and they soon know if they are safe in certain people's company. A safe, predictable, calm environment will be a sound base for building the early foundations of a positive internal narrative and increased Resilience in a young child.

Shame and poor attachment patterns also play a major part in how a child constructs the story of their life. However, I want to focus more on how you can use Transformative Communication to aid your child in creating a strong internal narrative and build their Resilience rather than dwell too much on why it might not be there. For now, I will simply recommend John Bradshaw's book, *Healing The Shame That Binds You* (1988), for more extensive information about shame. Bradshaw details how a child can become shamed from a young age and how a child displays shame throughout their stages of development. For more on attachment, I recommend anything by John Bowlby or Donald Winnicott.

The messages a child receives about themselves through direct communication, subtle communication, their place in their family and their experiences will lead to the thoughts and perceptions they have about themselves and the world around them. I refer to this as their 'internal narrative' because it is the story a child tells themselves about their life and the world around them, the way they think they are treated and whether they expect good or bad things to happen to them. This narrative is constantly growing and operates at a subconscious level. Improving it via Transformative Communication underpins the approach I promote in schools and with parents.

If the internal narrative of a child—or an adult for that matter—is generally positive, that person will have positive thoughts that lead to positive feelings which, if repeated, become firm positive beliefs that they have about themselves as they grow. They will be Resilient and believe that they can overcome challenges, because their story tells them so. Unfortunately, the same is true in reverse. A child who has repetitive negative thoughts, perceptions and feelings can develop fixed negative/toxic beliefs. That child is then highly likely to have a poor internal narrative, and this has a negative impact on their Resilience and subsequently their behaviour—the behaviour being a direct translation of their toxic beliefs.

The way a child views themselves is intrinsically linked to their levels of Resilience, and vice-versa.

Limiting/toxic beliefs

Here is an insight into thoughts and perceptions that become fixed beliefs for children who have a negative internal narrative and are lacking Resilience. The following list comes from children I have worked with and covers the most common kinds of limiting/toxic beliefs:

- I can't do it
- I'd rather not try than try and fail

- What is the point?
- What if …? (imagining the worst-case scenario)
- I should be able to …
- I struggle with …
- I am naughty/bad
- I need to comply
- I need to impress others
- Nobody likes me/Everybody hates me
- I am stupid
- The world is a scary place
- I'm not good enough

Just taking the first belief as an example, a child thinking *I can't do it* in certain situations is not too problematic. That child might have calmly assessed a situation and come to a sensible decision that they cannot indeed do whatever 'it' is! However, when *I can't do it* becomes a fixed belief, combined with the toxic feelings that come with that belief, it infiltrates every area of that child's life. Limiting and toxic beliefs quickly become part of the automatic story a child tells themself; the child is unwittingly conditioning themself to expect the worst. That child is then likely to demonstrate survival (negative) behaviours in a subconscious attempt to wrestle back control, leading to a negative response from an adult, further damaging their internal narrative. And so a vicious cycle ensues.

Behaviours that indicate a poor internal narrative and lack of Resilience

Let's look, then, at the behaviours that are a direct translation of a child's toxic beliefs and indicative of having a negative internal narrative and a possible lack of Resilience. These behaviours tend to fall into two different categories: rebellious and non-rebellious.

The seemingly rebellious child is likely to translate their negative internal narrative through the following behaviours:

- *Giving up easily.* If a child gives up 'on their own terms', they do not have to feel the pain of trying and failing—someone who has negative thoughts about themself simply cannot cope with such distress, as they perceive that failure affirms their belief that they are not good enough.
- *Will not attempt work.* When you are wracked with self-doubt, it is much safer not to try than to try and fail. Failure is like a dagger to the heart of a child who struggles with negative self-talk. An adult can try to tell a child that making mistakes is part of learning, but if that child's belief system says otherwise, they will not take on such information. (More on how an adult could positively address negative behaviours in Chapter 4.)
- *False confidence.* Similar to the false Resilience I mentioned earlier in this chapter, I often hear in response to my assertion that a child lacks confidence, "Well, he didn't lack confidence when he smirked at me at break time when I was talking to him about his behaviour." Other professionals report a child shouting, hurting someone, controlling a situation inappropriately or telling someone to shut up as evidence of confidence. Read that list of behaviours again. Would a *truly* confident child do any of those things? A child with a poor internal narrative uses false confi-dence as a bulletproof vest, as they think it guards them against the paralysing reality that they are viewed (and view themselves) as being the fragile and vulnerable person that, deep down, they know they are.
- *Disproportionate emotions.* Ever heard your child scream and go so red you think their face is about to pop when you have told them the only flavour of crisps left is cheese and onion? This is a disproportionate response. Normally, this happens to children with a negative narrative, as they cannot cope with even seemingly minor disappointments, because these disappoint-

ments only confirm the horrible story they tell themselves. Children who show these types of responses have an almost magnetic quality for negativity to prove that it is 'the world out there' that is making their lives hard!

- *Blaming others.* In schools I often hear that a child needs to 'take responsibility' for their behaviour. Imagine for a moment you feel weak, unloved, not liked, judged, stupid, ugly, invisible and unheard. Really put yourself in that position. Pictured it yet? Now take responsibility for a mistake you made while feeling all of these horrible things. Oh, and you're seven years old! It simply won't happen. A child with a poor internal narrative will blame someone or something else, because admittance of a mistake, to them, means they are the worst of the worst. They don't see 'taking responsibility'; they see 'taking the blame', or blame's twin sibling, feeling that the matter in question is their 'fault'. This simply confirms their worst fears: that they are a terrible person.
- *Distracting or ruining things for others.* If someone else messes something up, it takes the attention away from the person with the negative narrative.
- *Controlling behaviours.* This is one of the hardest and least endearing behaviours for adults to deal with. A child with low Resilience will try to control through behaviour, as they do not trust themselves or the world around them and have to create a world that is 'just so'. They will fight to keep their comfort zone as small and specific as possible, because edging out of it is unthinkable. A child may also use control to get what they want because of a perceived lack of Resilience, unaware that they have qualities and strengths to achieve their desired outcomes positively and without the need to control through behaviour.
- *Lying.* The reality the child lives is not what they want, so they lie to make themself more interesting, likeable, etc. When a child lies to get themself out of trouble, this comes back to being unable to take responsibility for something that has gone wrong (as touched on in the example regarding blaming).

Not all children with negative internal narratives are rampaging their way through homes, schools and parks like Sly Stallone on Skittles. The non-rebellious child shows their self-doubt and perceived lack of Resilience in the following ways:

- *Cries easily (often a quiet cry).* Different to the disproportionate responses I detailed earlier, a quiet, shy child may cry so quietly that an adult doesn't even notice. They do not want to draw attention to themselves, as the story they tell themselves is that they are weak and vulnerable.
- *Keeping a low profile.* An introverted child who struggles with confidence tends to see themself negatively, so why would they want to draw attention to themself and, in turn, all of their perceived hang-ups?
- *Very quiet.* A child who is anxious and withdrawn does not think anyone wants to hear what they have to say, and they may have experienced this (either perceived or real experience) in their lives. So keeping quiet is a survival mechanism.

Some behaviours that indicate a negative internal narrative and lack of Resilience occur whether a child falls into the rebellious or non-rebellious category:

- *Tummy aches and headaches.* A child who is anxious and negative will be in 'fight or flight' mode all too often. This causes cortisol and adrenaline spikes, as well as the likelihood that the child will hold themself for long periods in a contorted manner. This combination notoriously leads to tummy aches and headaches, sometimes causing the child to be sick. Another reason a child will tell an adult they have a physical ailment is because they know it will normally result in a nurturing and positive response from the adult—something they might not otherwise receive.

- *One setback ruins the whole day.* A child with a poor narrative will dwell on a setback and believe that the setback reinforces all the negative things they think about themself. They are not over the first setback when along comes another one. In these circumstances, I see children lurch from one crisis to another (more on this in 'The child's emotion scale', Chapter 4).
- *Sabotaging their own work, play and experiences.* Has your child ever screwed up their homework and thrown it across the table? Or quietly pressed down on the paper too hard so the pen or pencil rips the paper? Usually, this is because the child is so self-critical that they convince themself that what they are producing, much like themself, isn't good enough. They don't recognise their ability and strength to communicate the problem, so they take control, negatively, through sabotaging behaviour. Additionally, if they screwed the work up, they ended the activity on their own terms. A less rebellious child may sabotage their work, play or experiences more subtly, but they still do it.

All of the behaviours listed are what I refer to as 'survival behaviours'. Children use them for short-term benefit and/or as a defence mechanism. However, these behaviours do not help a child sustainably change their narrative. When an adult responds negatively to these behaviours, this simply reaffirms the negative narrative a child has about themself, and so they are likely to go on to display another survival behaviour—it is easy to get into a vicious cycle. Remember:

INTERNAL NARRATIVE → LEVEL OF RESILIENCE → BEHAVIOUR

What happens when negative thoughts and cycles are not dealt with?

Continued negative thoughts lead to negative feelings; repetition of this can lead to a child developing firm negative (sometimes toxic) beliefs that become stuck and immovable. Perception is king or queen in this situation; a sensitive child who has developed a negative belief system may become so conditioned to negativity that they perceive negative messages that are either not intended or simply not there. This can lead to conflict, as when a child articulates their sometimes-inaccurate perception, the adult with them may strongly disagree and focus on what they see rather than what the child is trying to tell them.

It is often the case that a child is trying to communicate something via their behaviour and body language. An adult can miss this, as the child's behaviour is at odds with what the adult needs from them at that moment in time. For example, imagine a child is taking too long to get ready for school, and the parent is worried about being late, and subsequently late for work. The child is anxious because they have a maths test, but they do not believe they can articulate this, so they try to control the situation via behaviour. The adult is already stressed, as they are worried about financial issues or relationship problems, or they haven't slept well, etc. Can you see that neither the parent nor the child's needs are being met here? What compounds this situation for the child is that the parent will typically criticise their behaviour rather than look beyond it to empathise with them. And so, an adult's negative response to behaviour can unwittingly play a part in damaging a child's internal narrative and Resilience further.

In Chapter 4, I will detail how to look beyond the behaviour and connect with the emotion or perceived problem that is driving it. Until then, let us assume that a child who lacks Resilience has sat in the vicious cycle depicted in Chapter 1, with all the negativity that comes with it, for some time. When a child is in a constant state of self-doubt, what follows are feelings of weakness and vulnerability. While these weaknesses and vulnerabilities can present themselves in many different ways, a young person making decisions from this standpoint can attract problems. Here are a few brief examples of what such problems may look like:

Falling into the 'wrong crowd'

How many times have you heard the old adage, 'they fell in with the wrong crowd'? Often this is down to a young person seeking external gratification from an inappropriate source because they simply do not like themself or their life and do not recognise their strengths that could help them overcome these restrictive feelings. The sense of belonging that the young person gets from being part of a crowd gives them something that is missing, even if that crowd displays negative behaviours.

Self-harm

It is important to distinguish between a young person reacting angrily and head-butting a wall and a young person who is seemingly calm but takes themselves away and intentionally harms themself. The latter is the ultimate expression of a lack of worth; the young person has reached a point at which they are punishing themself for being 'them'. Some young people also enjoy the healing aspect of self-harm; watching something heal and repair is a gratifying experience, so they recreate the damage in order to watch it heal again.

Isolation and withdrawal from family

A young person could feel so disconnected from their family, and perhaps feel so unwanted, that they choose to spend more and more time on their own. This gives them more time to ruminate on how bad they think they are, and their issues become worse.

Eating disorders

Using food to serve an emotional need of any kind is the seeking of gratification or punishment from an external source, as the young person does not like who they see themself as being.

Body image issues

The way someone views themself and their levels of Resilience are inextricably linked. A poor view of yourself can lead to any number of the issues detailed here, but it is not just how a child views themself internally that is problematic; the prevalence of social media and the global imagery of women with 'perfect' bodies and men with six-packs and muscles bulging out of their shirts has led to unrealistic role models for young people. This has put extra pressure on the young generation to live up to such images, particularly if a young person already thinks and feels negatively about themself. The faulty thinking of someone with a poor internal narrative is, *If I feel awful about myself, looking good will solve the problem.*

Inappropriate experimentation with drugs and alcohol

Many young people will experiment with drugs or alcohol during their teenage years, and this does not necessarily always lead to long-standing problems. However, when a young person struggles with their view of themself, doesn't like themself and gets exasperated with their perpetual state of low mood, they are more likely to seek to change their state via various substances and/or alcohol. A young person can then become reliant on drugs and/or alcohol as their only means of feeling 'better'.

Forging damaging relationships

During my career I have worked with many parents who go from one damaging relationship to another. They are in an inflated version of the negative cycles of thinking and feeling that children go through, and these patterns of behaviour will have been set at an early age. People stuck in this cycle seek 'anyone' to make them feel important, as they don't believe they *are* important. They allow themselves to be in a damaging relationship, because subconsciously they don't believe they are worthy of anything else, and the thought of going it alone when you have such a negative view of yourself is petrifying. If that person has a partner who tells them negative things about themselves, this reinforces their negative narrative and means they are unlikely to leave, as they think, *who else will have me?* When one damaging relationship breaks down, someone who thinks of themself as, and feels, vulnerable will broadcast this to the outside world through their body language and ways of interacting, thus attracting another partner similar to the last one. These patterns can be predetermined by a negative internal narrative in a person's formative years.

Failing to fulfil academic potential

Education professionals often say to me, "It is a real shame, because he is a bright boy. If only he could stop behaving so badly and knuckle down, he'd be fine." This misses the whole point. If only a child could feel strong, worthy, know their attributes, overcome their fear of failure and become Resilient, then they would be fine. Fulfilling academic potential does not happen when a child lacks Resilience. As Marci Shimoff writes in Happy for No Reason (2008), 'Success is not the key to happiness. Happiness is the key to success.' Similarly, academic achievement is not the key to a positive internal narrative; a positive internal narrative is the key to academic achievement. Trying to take short cuts, missing the need for building Resilience and focussing on the firefighting of poor behaviour only exacerbates the problem.

Issues with anger

I have a problem with the term 'anger management'. It is a sticking plaster when a major operation is needed. No matter how many times you tell someone who does not like themselves to breathe and count to ten, they will still get angry. Anger is linked to how you feel about yourself; it is easy to blame an external circumstance or person for your anger, but thinking and feeling negatively about yourself is what causes it. For example, how is it that some people can be cut up in traffic and calmly wave and let the person through, but another person will be in an aggressive frenzy about the same circumstance? It is down to how that person interprets the situation, and the more negative your view of yourself, the more you are likely to think that the world (or in this case, the other driver) is 'out to get you'.

Gender confusion

I have worked with many children who lacked regard for themselves, had nothing positive to say about themselves and were deeply unhappy. The answer to this for two of those children was to become the opposite sex. In both cases I encouraged the parents and education professionals involved with these children to build their internal narrative before taking any permanent action. In both cases the child lacked confidence, feared failure, said things like "I wish I was dead", felt unloved and unheard and didn't recognise any of their strengths—all classic signs of a poor internal narrative. How can a child who feels this way make a decision on their gender? Simply changing gender would not change the negative beliefs they had about themselves. In both cases, when each child felt more positive about themself and had more Resilience, they could then decide from a position of strength that they did or did not want to change their gender. I must note that if a child has had extensive support on improving their internal narrative and they still want to explore changing their gender, it is vital that they are supported through this process—however challenging that might be for the people around them.

Case study: I am the problem

(NB I have changed the names and some of the details of the people at the heart of this case study to protect the anonymity of the people involved.)

HK was adopted at four years of age by a loving couple who could not have children of their own. Up until that point in his life, HK had lived with several foster parents who had always tried their best to give him a safe and warm home. However, safety and warmth are only two of the absolute necessities a child needs in their formative years. They also need unconditional love, nurturing and an understanding of who they belong to and with. HK had none of these upon arrival at his new 'forever family'. It is safe to say, then, that HK was still trying to figure out his place in the world. Initially, things went well for HK and his new family. He was accepted by his new grandparents, aunties and uncles and went on holidays he would have only dreamed of previously. He played happily outside in the summer, kicked the leaves in the autumn and built snowmen in the winter. All seemed good in the world. As time went by, however, HK sporadically displayed flashes of anger that alarmed his adoptive parents. He changed schools and at age nine still had many unanswered questions about how he had come to live with several different people rather than his biological parents. Questions persisted: "Why did they not keep me?", "Was I not enough for them to change?", "Why did I have to adjust so many times?".

HK's adoptive parents tried their best to answer his questions, and on an intellectual level he kind of understood. But understanding on an intellectual level and understanding on a deeper, belief-based level are two very different things. Without realising it, HK had some toxic 'core beliefs'—beliefs that came from repeated thoughts, feelings, experiences and messages (perceived or actual, implicit or explicit). So these beliefs were stuck in his gut and deep in his subconscious. As such, rational explanations alone were not going to make him feel sustainably better. As time progressed, HK's outbursts became more violent towards his parents. To make things worse, there were times when he appeared calm but still hurt those closest to him, walking away with a seemingly cold smile on his face. HK would threaten, intimidate, negotiate and manipulate, all behaviours that are typically and understandably met with negative responses. Such responses only served to perpetuate the cycle, as HK interpreted the responses and stored more negativity into his internal narrative.

The strain on HK's adoptive parents was huge, and they confided in me that they wondered if they had done the right thing by adopting him. The relationship was on the verge of breaking down, and more and more professionals were getting involved, all with little impact. During a session with HK, I asked what his thoughts were about what was happening and how he felt about so many agencies speaking to him. He picked out one intervention where he and his parents had sat together with a professional and completed a form of mediation. He pondered, "Why were we all there?"

I told HK that one of the challenges he faced was that his relationship with his adoptive parents was not going very well, and whenever a relationship is suffering, it is never down to one person, but every person in the relationship. I added, "It is not just you who is the problem."

HK's response upset me and highlighted the deep-rooted negative beliefs he held about himself as he said, "Yes, but that is it, isn't it? I AM THE PROBLEM. They don't want me. They are just looking after me because they have to, and when I am old enough, they will throw me out. They don't love me. So I *am* the problem, aren't I?"

For a young person to view themselves like this is

heartbreaking. This view had built up over his life and gone unchecked. HK's adoptive parents had adopted him with the intention of giving him a home, a family, nurture, unconditional love and happiness. HK's responses had become so extreme that they now doubted they could keep him. HK picked up on this through their body language and non-verbal communication, and this made his story of self-hate all the more real. The more he felt like this, the more he pushed his adoptive parents away, and the cycle continued. The other case studies in this book are a lot more positive, but I wanted to include this one as a cautionary tale of how a negative internal narrative can cause such destruction. On a more positive note, HK is still with his adoptive parents, and he is accessing support through a number of agencies. While he still has regular emotional crises, I hope that the family are through the hardest part of what has been a hugely challenging time.

CHAPTER 3

Superpowers: The Foundation of Transformative Communication

I sit opposite 'Joe', a Year 6, eleven-year-old child with lots of friends, a lovely personality and great sporting prowess. I ask him, "What do you like about yourself?" He looks at me as if I have spoken in a different language and might have gone a bit mad. The look he gives me is one I have experienced seven times this week from various children. I venture another question: "If I asked the people who know you best, what would they tell me are your biggest strengths?"

Joe squirms in his chair, shrugs his shoulders, laughs and says, almost pleadingly, "I don't know!"

The interaction with Joe illustrates a big problem that exists within young people: they are brilliant, bright, creative and Resilient, but they do not have an inkling that they possess such strengths. When I am asked to work with a child, whatever the surface-level reason is, what I tend to see is a young person controlling situations via their behaviour (as discussed extensively in the previous chapter) rather than their skills. But if a child doesn't know what their skills are, how can they use them to control situations? This brings me to the foundation of the Transformative Communication approach I promote in schools and with parents to form the beginnings of an improved internal narrative. What follows will create the bedrock of any success you have from embedding the strategies suggested in this book; making your child more aware of their Superpowers.

Developing a more positive internal narrative through Superpower language

How does a child know anything about themselves? They are told, or they perceive through messages, interactions and experiences. So, in order for your child to become more aware of their strengths, you will have to tell them that they possess such strengths and detail how they use them on a regular basis. I am not referring to 'pep talks'; they give a temporary boost to a child who has a poor internal narrative. I am talking about inputting specific language about specific skills that your child has into as many interactions as possible. Here is how:

a) Draw up a list of Superpowers

Draw up a list of strengths you think your child has but may be unaware of. Look for skills you know will help serve them as they grow up. By skills and strengths, I mean things about their personality that you like and that will help them in a challenging situation. To give you some ideas, here is a breakdown of age-appropriate skills to talk about, dependent on the age of your child.

Superpowers of children aged between four and seven years old: Helpfulness, independence, calming down, caring, listening, determination, talking to a grown-up, creativity, imagination, cheerfulness.

Superpowers of children aged between eight and thirteen years old: Resilience, resourcefulness, independence, determination, problem-solving skills (if that feels a bit forced, then an alternative is 'finding a solution'), communication, self-control, trustworthiness, organisation, adaptability, perseverance, enthusiasm, focus, gratitude and empathy.

This is not an exact science and depends on how articulate your child is. You can use some words from the younger category with an older child, and vice-versa. Don't be discouraged if you think your child won't understand a word you have said; simply explain what it means and use it in context on repeat, gently reminding them of the meaning of that word each time.

b) Choose five strengths for incorporation into everyday language

Now choose five strengths from your list that you think you can realistically incorporate into everyday language with your child. For the purpose of giving you a clear idea of how to use this language, let's imagine you have chosen independence, problem-solving skills, determination, self-control and adaptability. In the brief sections below are some examples of how to input such Superpower language for everyday use.

In the moment
"Joe, I noticed you got on <u>independently</u> and showed real <u>determination</u> there with your homework."

Retrospectively
"I meant to say earlier, when you were playing with your Lego, that you showed brilliant <u>problem-solving skills</u> when you couldn't find the piece you were looking for." This use of language is useful if you feel like you have missed an opportunity to use Superpower language. This is likely to happen as you get used to trying to use the technique. Retrospective Superpower language means you will not miss opportunities as often.

Pre-emptively (before the event)
Imagine your child is going to an event that is out of their comfort zone. You can pre-empt the skills they can show to help them see that

they can make a positive impact. For example, you could say, "You are really <u>adaptable,</u> like when you got used to how different school was when you went back after the big break. You can adapt to this situation too." Adding evidence of how and when they have shown the skill required in previous situations helps the child believe they have that skill and that you are not simply trying to make them feel better. Use of pre-emptive Superpower language can be used in everyday scenarios and might make potentially challenging situations better. For example, your child drags their feet when they are supposed to be getting ready in the morning. You can say, "Okay, my <u>independent</u> girl, your clothes are on your bed. Show your <u>independence</u> and get ready ..." and then leave the conversation on that positive note. The use of pre-emptive Superpower language is not exclusive to challenging situations; it can be used as a prompt to your child what-ever they are about to do. For example, you could say, "You'll have to show those <u>problem-solving skills</u> in your maths homework" or "Let me see your <u>listening skills;</u> there is something we need to talk about".

Speculatively
You are not with your child all the time, so there will be times when they show skills you do not see. This doesn't stop you from speculating as to which skills they have shown when you were not with them. For example, when your child comes back from school and says they got a certificate for good handwriting, you can say, "Amazing, you must have shown a lot of <u>determination</u> to get that certificate." You can also use speculative Superpower language when a child has a grievance about something you didn't witness. For example, your child comes back from a club and says that someone really upset them by making fun of them. You can speculate as to which skills they must have shown to get through that situation by saying, for example, "You must have shown brilliant <u>problem-solving skills</u> and <u>self-control</u> to keep going and carry on with the activities." (NB I will talk a lot more about how you deal with a child who reports something negatively in Chapter 4.)

c) Making a start

You now have ideas of how and when to use Superpower language, the starting point of Transformative Communication. Dependent on your child, you may well tell them you are going to start using the language, particularly if you think they will be suspicious of you if, unannounced, you start talking in a different way! If you do talk to your child beforehand, I recommend saying something like the following: "Dad and I have been talking, and we notice that you are showing lots of skills as you get older. In fact, these skills are like your very own Superpowers! We notice that you show [insert five skills], but you don't always seem to know you are showing these Superpowers. It might feel a bit strange to hear these things about yourself, but we will still tell you when you are showing your Superpowers, because we think it is important." This is also a good opportunity to elaborate on what certain skills mean if you think that your child doesn't understand. I have encouraged some families to extend this activity further by having visual representations of the skills around the house; this varies from simple laminated cards with the Superpowers written on being stuck on the fridge, to photos of that child showing those Superpowers (perhaps more applicable for a younger child).

As you adapt to using Superpower language, you will find a way that works for you.

Overcoming barriers

Over years of using this approach, patterns tend to emerge. I can use such patterns to anticipate pitfalls and barriers to seeing optimal results from Superpower language. To ensure the language doesn't hit barriers straight away, there are seven additional tips listed on page 28:

- *Try your best not to sound surprised when you are using Superpower language.* Children pick up on subtle communication cues, and if they sense you are stunned to see them showing a Superpower, they will know you are trying to convince yourself as well as them!
- *Don't use Superpower language in a way that makes it obvious to the child that you have an ulterior motive.* Children tend to know when you are using positive language to cajole them and will subsequently reject the language. I've known parents and education professionals who draw up daily checklists to ensure children show their Superpowers; this is a breeding ground for the child to feel like they are 'failing' to use their Superpowers should they not tick each one off the list. Alternatively, they could show the Superpowers purely to avoid the horrible feeling of what they see as failure.
- *Say what you say, then walk away!* A child with a poor inner voice can find it hard to hear positives about themselves. As such, most children do not want an audience after they have been praised. So be to the point, notice the Superpower that is relevant then walk away.
- *Keep it light and breezy.* Steer clear of the old adage that you have to get on your child's level and gain their eye contact to ensure they are listening to you. Of course, there is a time and place for that approach; however, when using Superpower language, your child may benefit if you talk about the Superpower they have shown as you are busy doing something (making a cup of tea, preparing dinner, driving).
- *Consider your tone.* Be clear, concise and matter-of-fact in tone while using Superpower language. Your child will feel more comfortable than if you used a 'cringey parent' voice, and you will probably feel more comfortable and less self-conscious when you do things this way. This will vary, dependent on the age of your child—some younger children like a bit of expression in their parent's voices!

- *Consider the age of your child.* Following on from the last point, it is not just your tone you have to consider when thinking about what is age-appropriate for your child. For example, some older children may understandably reject the notion of Superpowers. If you think this will be the case with your child, replace 'Superpowers' with 'Skills', 'Strengths' or 'Attributes'.
- *Superpowers > 'Good'.* Parents and teachers have regularly told me, "We are always telling her how good she is at maths" as evidence that they use Superpower language. The sad truth is that many children with a poor internal narrative use black-and-white thinking and cannot access the belief that they are 'good'. They see themselves quite crudely as 'bad'. So hearing that you are 'good' when you feel the opposite can induce a shameful feeling for that person. A child hearing, in context, that they are independent, adaptable, brave, determined and/or a problem-solver is more palatable and 'real'. While words like 'good', 'amazing', 'brilliant' and 'fantastic' are all well inten-tioned, they are too general and rarely mean a lot to a child with a negative inner voice. If these words are part of your everyday language, supplement them with Superpower language. For example, "Absolutely brilliant. You were really <u>independent</u> getting ready for school so quickly."

Some other common barriers preventing this approach getting off the ground can be found below, along with potential solutions to such issues.

i) The child says they do not like hearing Superpower language about themselves

This is an indicator that the child does not yet believe what you are saying about them. They have had years of practising negative thinking (more on negativity bias later), so perseverance is sometimes needed to develop a new internal narrative. Some empathy might be needed. So, for example, you could say, "I know this feels a bit uncomfortable, but you do have <u>problem-solving skills</u>, and I am very proud of you." Then walk away.

ii) The child winces when the parent praises them
This is similar to the first barrier. A child has built up a negative internal narrative and doesn't believe it when someone says something nice about them. Reiteration is needed, more so than with a child who seems to receive Superpower language straight away. As I mentioned earlier, the type of audience you are once you have used Superpower language is important. A shy child who lacks confidence will not want you to stand close to them, looking at them, after you have praised them. You can employ the 'say what you say, then walk away' or 'keep it light and breezy' tactics.

iii) A child cannot see that they have shown skills in other situations
Let's imagine your child is going to a party where they don't know anyone, and you have reminded them of another time they joined in with a group of people they didn't know. This type of approach can sometimes be met with, "Yeah, but that was different. I wanted to go there." Gentle reiteration is required here by perhaps saying, "I remember you were quite anxious, but you were really <u>adaptable</u> and <u>brave</u>, and these skills made that time okay for you. These same skills will help you again today."

iv) The child actively opposes the language
A child could perhaps respond to Superpower language with, "No, I don't have stupid problem-solving skills!" I will cover more on this in Chapter 4, but you could respond with something like, "I know you are angry and don't believe me, but you do have <u>problem-solving skills</u>." Then walk away. Do not get into an argument about the use of Superpower language by saying something like, "Well, I'm telling you, you do have problem-solving skills!" If your child is clearly not receptive at a particular moment,

empathise then walk away, and talk to them again when they have calmed down.

v) Lack of confidence/motivation on the part of the parent

Occasionally, because of any number of factors, a parent says, "I just can't do it." I will cover this issue in Chapters 5 and 6.

So why are we not more positive?

Marci Shimoff, author of *Happy for No Reason* (2008), states that we have 60,000 thoughts a day, 45,000 of which are negative! This is down to what Marci refers to as a 'negativity bias'—as a society, we are more negative than positive. Shimoff suggests this is because back in ancient times it paid to be wary, watchful and to assume the worst in order to survive. She goes on to suggest that happy people who relaxed and slept under the stars would be eaten! As we have evolved, our negativity bias hasn't. The media do not help, preying on our every insecurity to try to sell us solutions to our perceived or supposed problems.

To bring it back to everyday life, and give you an example I hope you can relate to, I will tell you about my own negativity bias. Before I became aware of just how often I complained and the damaging effects this can have, an interaction with my wife as I came back from work would go something like this:

My wife asks me, "How was your day?"

I tell her that the traffic on the way to one school was so bad that I was late, the head teacher gave me a raised eyebrow and now I think that he thinks I am unreliable (talk about a negative narrative!). I ignore the fact that another head teacher praised me for the impact I have had at her school and thanked me for the advice I gave her regarding her teenage daughter that has made such a difference. I don't tell my wife about the little boy who went in the swimming pool without crying for the first time today, after the teacher used the

Transformative Communication strategies we have been working on for weeks. I fail to mention that a parent thanked me for my advice on how to get their child into their own bed and how successful the strategies have been. I tell my wife about the five per cent of my day that didn't go well, neglecting the ninety-five per cent that went really well. Does that sound familiar?

Children show strengths on repeat every minute of every day. However, many of our interactions with children are negative. We simply don't notice the skills (or Superpowers) that our child shows, because often we are not 'looking for' those skills. As mentioned earlier, a child is able to control situations via skills or behaviour. Typically, children control via their skills for the majority of the time, but in very unremarkable ways. Subsequently, adults do not draw attention to the skills shown; we just expect them to demonstrate the skills and often don't even recognise when this has occurred. For example, a child takes their pencils out of their pencil case in preparation for homework. Do we praise them for independence and being proactive? No, because we expect them to get pencils out. However, if a child controlled this situation by sitting with arms folded and pencil case zipped (behaviour), an adult may quickly draw attention to such behaviour. This feeds the negativity bias.

Trying to implement a more positive use of communication is also challenged by a social acceptance of negativity and a social scepticism of positivity. Think about our culture. People openly say, "We will get together and put the world to rights", meaning, "We will complain about everything we are unhappy about." On the other hand, we tend to think that being positive is 'weird' or 'cringey', often using humour alongside positivity so as not to be judged as strange. The sad truth is that positivity makes people uncomfortable.

Negativity is compounded by the amount of demands we make on children without knowing it. In *The Incredible Years* (2005 version), Carolyn Webster-Stratton states that the average parent gives seventeen commands to their child within a thirty-minute period.

Webster-Stratton goes on to add that within families where children have more behaviour problems, the number of commands per thirty minutes rises to forty! This is a lot for a child to process and explains why they will often switch off from a parent who uses too much dialogue, particularly when that dialogue is negative.

Negative cycles can easily develop: the child switches off from negative comments, the parent gets even more frustrated as they feel ignored and then the parent gives even more negative comments to their child! This plays a part in creating a negative internal narrative. I would suggest reducing the commands given to children, but also making the commands positive. For example, a parent could say, "Use your problem-solving skills and work independently on your homework for a few minutes while I make a start on dinner. I will be with you in a minute." This sets a clear expectation, and you have told your child about two Superpowers they can use to achieve this. I often talk to parents about developing a 'positivity radar'. This is like a game you play with yourself. Think of a symbol that represents positivity for you; it can be a colour, an object, an animal, a word, a smell—anything that means something to you. Whenever you experience this symbol, it is a prompt for you to think of something positive about your child right there on the spot. Even if you don't say out loud what you are thinking to start with, just becoming more aware of the positives your child brings to you will help you think more positively about them. You are much more likely to look for and acknowledge their skills if your brain is exposed to positive thinking about your child.

Summary

Introducing Superpower language changes a child's internal narrative and gives them a foundation upon which to build on. This part of my Transformative Communication approach is also critical to the next strategy; without Superpower language, the Empathy and

Empowerment strategy will not work. Superpower language helps a child identify with their strengths, and their Superpowers become part of who they see themself as being.

By becoming more aware of their skills, a child is more able to see that the skills *themselves* are what they can control. So, even if the outcome isn't what they desire, they can take something positive from the experience and learn something about themself to add to their internal narrative. This is an example of the positive Resilience I referenced earlier, and this learning is crucial for a child to then apply their skills to challenging situations. Like anything new, developing Superpower language can take some time for a parent to master. You will have to find a way that works best for you. While I have given you direction and some ideas of the dialogue you can use, it has to be authentically 'you' who is talking to, and with, your child.

Life can be stressful, particularly with children! Children can do things that directly conflict with an adult's needs at any moment in time. For example, you are in a rush, and they won't put their shoes on; you want some quiet time to get on with something, but they are arguing with a sibling; they won't go to bed ... The list could go on. These factors, along with the negativity bias I discussed earlier, present parents with challenges to being more positive. With all of this in mind, I am aware that the suggestions in this book are, for the majority of people, not typical ways of communicating. However, I have seen first-hand the impact these strategies have when applied consistently: improved relationships between parents and children, less negative flashpoints, children trying things out of their comfort zone (including trying new food!) and more patient parents. Most importantly, a child who has a more rounded inner voice is more likely to live a happy, healthy life as an adult.

Give yourself some care and understanding. If you have a bad day and shout at your child(ren), try again with the strategies tomorrow. In Chapters 5 and 6 I will give several suggestions that might help you 'get out of your own way' if you believe yourself to be the obstacle to the suggested strategies working. You are trying, and as

Les Brown (life coach, author and motivational speaker) says, "You don't have to be great to get started, but you do have to get started to be great."

Case study: I'll show my problem-solving skills

BD, a six-year-old boy with a soft and lovely side to his character, had a tendency to completely overreact to any disappointment. Previously, this had been met with exasperation and impatience by his parents, particularly his dad. Knowing something had to change, BD's dad started using Superpower language and had focussed on this for about two months. He replaced "Wait a minute!" with "Show your problem-solving skills, and I will come to you in a minute". While BD still had emotional crises, his dad had noticed a little bit more Resilience developing in BD and was encouraged that some positive change was occurring. It was the hot summer of 2018, and BD was playing with his brand-new World Cup Russia 2018 football he had got for his birthday. Dad was chopping up holly from a fallen tree and putting it in the bin for recycling. BD kicked the ball into the nettles in their garden. He looked to his dad and started to say, "Daddy, can you ...?" At this point, BD interrupted himself and said, "Don't worry, I'll show my problem-solving skills." BD's dad nearly collapsed right there in the garden! BD, without prompting, had recognised the Superpower he needed to show to solve the problem for himself.

BD proceeded to get a long stick and try to rake the ball out of the nettles. Proud and still amazed, dad looked over and noticed BD was really struggling to release the ball. He tiptoed into the nettles, got the ball and gave it to BD, along with a nurturing ruffle of his hair. He went on to tell BD how proud he was of him for showing his problem-solving skills, and BD beamed as he carried on playing football. Note that the desired outcome (getting the ball himself) hadn't been achieved, but BD was so happy to know he had shown a Superpower, he didn't worry. When the pair went in for lunch an hour or so later, BD held onto his dad's waist and said, "I love you, daddy." Pride in his heart, dad's day had been made.

Interestingly, when I asked BD's dad how the interaction would have gone had BD not been aware of his problem-solving skills, this is what he said would have happened: "He'd have asked me to get the football. I'd have said, 'Wait a minute' quite calmly the first time. By the fourth time I would have shouted, 'I said in a minute!', to which he would have stamped his feet, and his face would have gone red. He would still have tried to get the ball himself, but I would have been annoyed by his badgering and would have told him he was doing it wrong. Then I would have marched into the nettles, probably got stung, blamed him and launched the ball out to/at him. He would have cried and gone inside." You can see the vast difference in these two outcomes to the same scenario, simply by making a child more aware that he has a Superpower.

CHAPTER 4

Empathy and Empowerment: The Keys to Sustainable Change

We have established a solid foundation of Transformative Communication using Superpower language. This can help your child build more confidence and recognise skills as part of their identity. Parents often ponder that they understand it is important to be positive but wonder what they ought to say when their children do something wrong, seem upset, go through something difficult and/or let anxiety get the better of them. In this extensive chapter, we will look at how to use Transformative Communication to continue to build your child's internal narrative in seemingly negative situations—not just in response to negative behaviour, but to other challenges a child might face as well. In addition to negative behaviour, other situations and behaviours that are commonplace when a child has a negative internal narrative include; having disproportionate responses, refusing to complete a task, being anxious when a particular event has upset them and falling into an emotional crises. To help respond to such scenarios, in this chapter I will give details on how to use a specific technique that I call 'Empathy and Empowerment'.

Remember: INTERNAL NARRATIVE ➡ LEVEL OF RESILIENCE ➡ BEHAVIOUR

A negative internal narrative belies a child's lack of awareness of their strengths and how they can control situations positively. In fact, the negative self-talk that comes with a poor internal narrative has a damaging impact on that child's Resilience; they are unable to take responsibility for a mistake, resolve a conflict, overcome a setback

37

and/or complete tasks they perceive to be out of their comfort zone. When a child's Resilience is compromised, we tend to see them go into survival behaviours that are a direct translation of their inner voice. Here are a few examples of the inner voice communicating through behaviour:

SURVIVAL BEHAVIOUR	INNER VOICE
Sabotaging a sibling's play date.	I feel second best.
Lashing out.	I am really angry.
Having a tantrum when you suggest a family walk.	That isn't what I want to do.
Clinging to a parent at the school gate.	I don't think I can cope without you.
Refusal to do homework (1).	I'm fed up of work. I've been at school all day.
Refusal to do homework (2).	I am rubbish at maths.
Reluctance to go to a class party.	Nobody likes me.
False confidence/bravado.	Showing vulnerability means I am weak and stupid.
Blaming someone else for something they clearly did.	I know it was me, and that means I am horrible, terrible and unlovable, so I cannot admit it was me.

So often adults understandably focus on the surface-level behaviour without looking beyond the behaviour to the problem and/or emotion the child is communicating. Subsequently, when a child complains, blames, lashes out and avoids difficult challenges (examples of controlling situations with survival behaviour), the response that a child tends to get from an adult is not what they need—further supporting the negative view the child has about themselves.

Parents tend to fall into one of two categories in their response to the different kinds of negative situations and behaviours listed above: they either want to rescue their child, or they are negative, corrective, critical and/or demanding of their child. In other words, a parent can almost be too supportive or too challenging. By learning about the use of Empathy and Empowerment, you will see how you can be 'supportively challenging'—the dream Transformative Communication ticket in building a strong internal narrative and with it, Resilience. Once Resilience is established, behaviour will change. Some parents want behaviour to change before they start to use Transformative Communication; this is wishful thinking. A child will not change their behaviour until they feel more Resilient, and this can be achieved using the strategies suggested. Before I move on to how to implement Empathic and Empowering language, it is important to look at how negative cycles can develop when the challenges a child faces are handled by either rescue or criticism.

Let's start with a real example of a child being rescued and the negative impact this can have on their internal narrative. In this instance I will refer to the child as 'Child B'. Child B is about to go on a residential with school. This involves being away from home for three nights. She is anxious, doesn't want to go and is pleading with her parents not to 'make' her go. The parents are feeling guilty and just want their child to feel safe and happy. They suggest Child B only goes for one night, but if she really doesn't want to go, she doesn't have to go at all. When a child is given an 'out' from anxiety, they will always take it. Child B takes the 'deal' of possibly going on the residential for one night but tells everyone, "*I might* go, but only for one night." She is already gearing up to the next level of bargaining—not going at all! In this instance, Child B did not go on the residential. Initially, she felt relieved. Then, at school, the week after the residential, all of Child B's friends were talking about the fun they had. They had 'in' jokes, some had forged new friendships and they had all taken something positive from the experience that Child B had missed out on. At this point, Child B felt some regret at not being a part of the experience. She believed that anxiety, like an external intruder, had taken the opportunity away from her. She became a 'victim' of anxiety. Her narrative was, *If I didn't feel anxious, I could have gone.*

To compound the situation, it is possible that, when other challenges come along, Child B will have no reference point of success to look back on, because she didn't go on the residential. She is then highly likely to avoid challenges or seek reassurance and allowances before thinking about taking a challenge on.

Initially, Child B's behaviour (pleading, crying, desperation) translated an inner voice that said, *I am scared. I will not cope if I go away. I am weak and fragile.* On the face of it, going for one night rather than none seems like a good compromise. However, introducing this as an option only serves to tell Child B (indirectly and in an implied rather than explicit manner) that her negative inner voice is correct—she is someone who has a limitation, something that is stopping her from doing what her peers are doing. This now becomes a fixed part of her narrative. Remember earlier when I covered the beliefs of a child with a negative internal narrative? Specifically, the 'I struggle with ...' example? This 'rescuing' approach only reinforces the 'I struggle with ...' mentality of a child who is anxious. This, along with the thought, *If I didn't feel anxious, I could have gone,* are examples of how a child develops negative perceptions from implied (often unintended) messages from adults. If, as so often happens, these messages transfer into consistent thoughts, they will then be accompanied by consistent negative feelings and eventually convert into fixed negative beliefs. As discussed earlier, once this happens, the child builds up negative parts of the narrative they tell themselves and feel even more anxious. And so the cycle continues.

I will now cover the slightly different scenario whereby the parent criticises, corrects and dismisses their child. In this instance, the child will be referred to as 'Child X'. Child X feels down. He is worried his parents love his brother more than him. His brother is academically bright, funny, good at sport and has lots of friends. Child X feels that his parents have lots of positive interactions with his brother but only ever shout at him. Whether this is true or not, his perception is key to his thinking/believing. He dares not ask his parents if his fear is true, because he is scared of the answer and/or doesn't trust what they might say to reassure him. Child X's brother has a friend for a sleepover. He is happy and cheerful, having lots of fun with his friend. Feeling unheard, unloved and second best, Child X walks around the house being rude, grumpy and short with his parents. Eventually, tired of the attitude, the dad says to Child X, "What is wrong with you?"

Child X replies aggressively, "Nothing!"

Dad says, "Well clearly there is something. I'm trying to talk to your brother, and all I can hear is you slamming and huffing and puffing."

Child X, close to tears, shouts, "You always want to speak to *him*, don't you? It's always him. What about me?"

Dad says, "Don't speak to me like that. You've been moping around the house all day. You ought to count yourself lucky. Your brother is just getting on with his weekend. Why can't *you*?"

And so the cycle continues! I give these examples to illustrate how easy it is to create a negative cycle within your child, even when it is the parent's last intention.

How to use Empathic and Empowering language

In short, using Empathic and Empowering language means empathising with how your child is feeling by looking beyond surface-level behaviour to the inner voice being portrayed by that behaviour. You would then empower your child(ren) by talking about the Superpowers they can show, have shown or are already showing to positively influence the situation. When applied consistently, you will be transforming your child's internal narrative. Empathising with a child helps validate their feelings; they no longer feel 'silly' for feeling something negative. How often do you say or hear, "Don't be silly; it will be all right"? Well-meaning as this is, the child is essentially being told they are silly for feeling something negative—they could certainly perceive this, even if it is not the intention. We get caught up in trying to protect children from negative emotions. This is often a projection of our inability to deal with negative emotions as adults. By empathising calmly with a negative emotion, an adult is modelling to a child that such emotions are not to be feared.

On another note, when a child is behaving negatively, they are always trying to communicate a problem, emotion or both. Remember, negative behaviour is a direct translation of a child's negative beliefs about themselves. Empathising with what your child is trying to communicate, and/or how they feel, will lead to your child being more receptive to moving on positively.

Following empathy with empowering language helps a child know that no matter what the challenge, experience or event that is out of their control, they *can* control their response to it using their Superpowers. Children tend to base their level of positivity on the success of the outcome to a situation. However, brilliant as a child might be, not every situation has a positive outcome (remember BD and the ball in the nettles?)—that is not the world we live in! If a child can recognise, with the help of an adult, the skills, intention and purpose they have shown, they are more likely to learn something positive about themselves whatever the outcome, thus turning a challenge into an opportunity for learning positive Resilience. Please note that your child has to know about their skills before they believe they can use them in challenging situations. That is why the Superpower language strategy in the previous chapter has to be established for this one to work. In other words, do not only use positive language to try to help your child through a crisis; establish Superpower language for a week or so before attempting Empathy and Empowerment, then continue to use the strategies in the previous chapter alongside Empathy and Empowerment. One does not replace the other.

What follows is a guide to how you can implement Empathic and Empowering language into a number of different scenarios. Some examples require more detail than others, but I hope, in covering several situations I have come across in my career, the following sections have something for everyone to put into practice at home.

i) Responding to negative behaviour

In order to use Empathic and Empowering language in response to 'negative behaviour', it is important to look beyond the behaviour itself to the inner voice (the emotion, feeling or perceived negative belief a child has about themself that is driving the behaviour). This can be difficult for an adult, as the negative behaviour their child is showing might be linked to what the parent perceives as a failing on their part. Remember Child X from earlier? It would be difficult for his parent to acknowledge that the feeling driving Child X's behaviour was jealously because he thinks you love his sibling more. A parent's worry in situations like this can be alleviated somewhat by knowing that a child's perception is not always a fact. However, the child, whether through false perception or not, can feel strong and negative emotions. Their perception is true to them, and this needs to be acknowledged. So, the parent has to look beyond their own sensitivity and stay with their child's inner voice. Sticking with the Child X example, a parent can use Empathy and Empowerment by saying, "It must be horrible to feel like we always speak to your brother and don't do the same with you." (Note: 'to feel like' is a clever use of language, as it does not dismiss the feeling as not true, but neither does it confirm that Child X is 'right'.) His perception is taken seriously; this is the empathic part of the language. To add empowerment, the parent would say, "I'm glad you have been <u>brave</u> enough to tell me that this is what is bothering you. I want you to show <u>self-control</u> to <u>calm down</u>, and then we can do some <u>problem-solving</u> so you don't carry on feeling like this." Here the child hears what they can do, using their

Superpowers, and also that their parent will help them solve the problem. This is an example of how to 'supportively challenge' your child, as I referenced earlier.

ii) Responding to disproportionate responses

A specific example often helps me illustrate how to use the Transformative Communication I am encouraging. So, to exemplify how to deal with 'disproportionate responses', let's imagine your child has screamed, run to their room and thrown themselves onto their bed because you said they could not have a friend for a sleepover as you have other plans for that evening. Here, using Empathy and Empowerment would look like this: "I can see you are really upset and probably had the idea in your head that Tom could come for a sleepover. It is disappointing when you are excited about something and it doesn't happen. Use your self-control to calm down, and when you are ready, we can talk about arranging another time for Tom to come." Note that in the examples I am giving, I am not prompting you to justify *why* you have made a decision or acted in a certain way. In this example the parent has told their child why he cannot have a friend over before the child reacted disproportionately. Therefore, there is no need to explain this again. Your child will not listen, and at that point doesn't care! Stay with how your child is feeling and what they can positively do about it. An added bonus is that not justifying yourself will alleviate your own negative self-talk that might sound like, *Why am I justifying myself to my child?*

iii) Responding to a refusal to complete a task

Remember the list of behaviours in Chapter 2? Refusal to try something for fear of failing featured prominently in that list. This can apply to a child putting barriers up to doing homework, for example. Now, because this behaviour is in direct contrast to what you want to see from your child, it is easy to fall into the negative trap of labelling this behaviour as 'laziness', 'not willing to give things a go' and 'can't be bothered'. All of these labels will only add to the child's negative internal narrative, and they will be less likely than ever to try something they feel they might fail at. Another vicious cycle develops. Keep in mind that a child is usually trying to communicate something to you via their behaviour. So, if the child's inner voice is saying, *I am useless at maths*, imagine how much worse the inner voice will sound if it hears "lazy" and "can't be bothered" at that moment. Using Empathy and Empowerment, a parent would look past the behaviour and focus on the emotion or problem that is being communicated via the behaviour. Then, reference the skills/Superpowers the child has to overcome the challenge or negative feeling they are experiencing. An example of how to do this when your child is putting off or refusing to do their homework would be: "You've been at school all day, and the last thing you want to do now is more work. You probably just want to relax. I've heard you say you think you are terrible at maths. That must be horrible to feel like that. I know that, with your <u>determination</u>, you can give it a go <u>independently</u>." If your child says they think they can't do it, the empathy might be: "I notice you really don't like the feeling you have when you think you have failed. It must be difficult to feel so bad about it." Then mention problem-solving skills and independence with the caveat that you will be back in a few minutes to help if needed. This is another example of supportively challenging your child. I am aware that every refusal will not be linked to a fear of failure; more mundane activities—like putting their shoes on, getting ready in the morning, going to bed at night, etc.—are classic times when a child will refuse to do what you are asking of them. The same strategy applies: empathise then empower! So, if they refuse to get ready in the morning, you can say, "I know you have other things you would rather do, and you are a bit tired. I want you to show the <u>independence</u> I know you have, and I keep talking about, to get yourself ready as quickly as possible. Good lad. Thank you."

iv) Responding to anxiety

Anxiety is becoming increasingly prevalent in children. Since March 2021, eighty-two per cent of my one-to-one referrals mention anxiety as a significant factor for referring the child. With this in mind, I am going to cover two examples of how to use Empathic and Empowering language in response to two different presentations of anxiety.

Firstly, let me take you back to Child B and her avoidance of the school residential. I set the scene earlier, so let us move on to how to use Empathic and Empowering language. Remember, Child B's inner voice was saying, *I am scared. I will not cope if I go away. I am weak and fragile.* This has to be acknowledged, however unpleasant it might be for Child B's parents. So, Child B's parents might say, "I know you are scared, and don't think you can cope being away without us. I see you are feeling anxious, and it cannot be easy to feel like you do now." Empathy established, it is crucial that Child B is not allowed to use this an opportunity to wallow, so I would recommend quickly adding, "You are <u>brave</u>. You go to school every day, even though you don't like being away from us. You are a <u>problem- solver</u>. I've never seen you give up in maths, even when I haven't understood your homework! I see how you have <u>adapted</u> to Dad and I separating, even though it has been hard for you. All of these Superpowers can help you while you are away." By adding evidence of when Child B has shown the relevant Superpowers previously, she will see that this is not just a 'pep talk' designed to make her go. She is hearing about the transferrable skills she has that would undoubtedly help her should she go away with school.

The story doesn't end there for Child B and her parents. In the build up to the residential, they will have to continue to tell Child B when she is showing adaptability, problem-solving, courage, determination, independence, self-control—all Superpowers that will help her overcome anxiety. Child B's parents would also need to show Child B pictures of the place she will be staying at and use language like *"When* you go on your residential" as opposed to *"If* you go on your residential", thus setting the positive expectation that she will go away as planned.

Using the strategies suggested above, Child B's inner voice would be transformed to, *I am anxious about going away, and that is okay. My Superpowers are much stronger than my worries. I will face this, and with my determination, problem-solving, independence and courage, I will go on my school residential whether I am anxious or not.* Maybe the language won't be quite the same, but hopefully you understand the point I am making!

It is easy for a parent to become exasperated with a child who feels anxious to the degree that it stops them from doing seemingly everyday activities. Think about a child who feels significant anxiety; not just when they are going on a residential, but whenever they separate from a particular parent. In this case, it is likely that anxiety will affect many areas of the child's life. However, anxiety will become more acute in certain specific situations. For example, going to a club like gymnastics, Cubs or drama. I have worked with children who have insisted they would only go to a club if their parent stayed throughout the time. In some cases this was not typical, as no other parents stayed to watch their child. Even when the parent attended clubs, the child would usually spend the entire session looking out to check that their mum or dad had not left and trying to mouth messages to them. Continuing with this example, in the days before drama, gym or Cubs, the child with separation anxiety got agitated and wanted regular reassurance that their parent would attend their activity and would not leave. Often a parent thinks that staying during the activity is the right thing to do to appease their child. After all, the parent tells themself that it is better than the child not going at all! However, no matter how many times the parent stays at drama, gym or Cubs, their child's anxiety will remain high in anticipation for the next week. By going to drama every week, however well intentioned, the parent is giving their child the message that it is reasonable to expect them to stay, and that without their parent being there, the child cannot cope.

So, how can we solve this problem using Empathic and Empowering language? Firstly, if you have a child who feels anxious regularly, it is important to use Empathic and Empowering language in response to any anxiety your child shows: going to school, going to bed, going to a friend's house and general separations from their parent. Using Empathic and Empowering language regularly in response to anxiety will start to give your child messages that they are heard, validated and cared for, while also knowing that their skills are greater than their anxiety—so we are not just tackling the 'big one' (i.e. going to drama). In order for a child to think, feel then believe that their skills are greater than their anxiety, they will have to be exposed to this approach many times. I would also encourage the parent in this situation to set up small separations that might provoke a little anxiety, then use Empathic and Empowering language. For example: "I am just going to the shop. Dad is here and will watch you for a few minutes." If that is greeted by an anxious response, the parent could say, "I can see you are anxious, but you can work through this using your <u>problem-solving skills</u>. Dad is here to talk to, and I will be back shortly." When mum returns from the shop, however anxious and upset the child seems, it is crucial that they are acknowledged as being brave and that the situation is 'celebrated' as a victory. The child's upset does not mean the experiment was a failure; it highlights to the child, *I was upset and anxious, but I got through that, and everything is okay now.*

Using Empathic and Empowering language to tackle anxiety in several situations gives a child reference points regarding how they are successfully dealing with anxiety on a day-to-day basis. When this is established, the parent can then tackle the event that seems to cause the child the most acute anxiety (sticking with the example used, going to drama, gym or Cubs). With any child who is anxious, it is important not to simply throw them into the proverbial deep end unexpectedly. I recommend that a day before the child is due to go to the club that causes them so much anxiety, the parent has the following conversation: "Jack, tomorrow I am going to drop you off at drama and come back after twenty minutes, as I have a few jobs I need to do." (Expect pleading, upset and "I'm not going!" at this point.) "I know you are upset and worried, but you are <u>strong</u> and <u>determined</u> too. You are <u>committed</u> to going to drama. You have brilliant <u>self-control</u>. Look how you have managed going to school every day, even when you have felt really anxious. You are so <u>brave</u>." This approach, coupled with lots of TLC, may not alleviate the child's anxiety, but it will create an expectation that they are still going to drama and that they have the tools to cope with that. More tears and upset may follow, but reiteration of the Empathic and Empowering language is key.

Anxious children get really skilled at behaving in a way that gets them out of doing what they don't want to do! But allowing them to avoid anxious situations simply reinforces their negative internal narrative of, *If I can get out of this, I will be okay*. By creating an expectation that the child will come through an anxiety-provoking situation, feeling that they have been empathised with, understood and with a new-found awareness of the Superpowers they will need to show, the child will start to form a new narrative that looks a lot more like, *Although I might feel anxious, I can do this*. How much better does that sound?

The next most heart-rending and painful part of the process is absolutely crucial. As a parent, you have to see it through. Staying with the example I have used here, this means leaving the drama/gym studio, whether your child is crying or not. Use your judgement in these situations, perhaps ringing ahead and letting the professional in charge know what you are doing and why. They can then be prepared for any issues that will follow. Over time, the parents I have worked with, in situations like those illustrated here, could leave their child not just for twenty minutes, but the whole hour. It is the initial tearing of the metaphorical plaster that is challenging. Please do not judge the success of this approach on the complete eradication of anxiety. That is unlikely to happen. This approach helps a child deal with anxiety positively. Hopefully, this gives parents of anxious children some tools to use.

Before moving on, I'd like to mention a seemingly small detail that can unintentionally exasperate anxiety within a child. I often hear people say, "I *have anxiety*" or "My child *has* anxiety" or "He couldn't go because of *his* anxiety". This terminology gives the impression that the anxiety belongs to the person who is feeling it. It is difficult to rid yourself of something that belongs to you. Be careful not to use this type of language with or around a child who regularly feels anxious. Replace "My child has anxiety" with "My child feels anxious sometimes, and he is working to overcome this". Replace "He couldn't go because of his anxiety" with "He didn't go, but we will work on going next time". It is easy to build anxiety into a 'big bad wolf' that has a grip on a child, and this can become part of their narrative.

v) Responding to an event that has upset your child

As I mentioned in Chapter 2, children with a negative internal narrative will often report things negatively. They might blame and be critical of other people. When an event occurs that everyone would agree is difficult for a child, they will report it in a fashion that paints them as being a 'victim'. Parents can unintentionally feed negative narratives in two distinct ways: by simply joining in with the blaming and complaining, or by dismissing what the child has said—"I'm sure it wasn't that bad." These two types of responses have different effects, neither of which help the child develop a stronger narrative. Joining in with the blaming and complaining reinforces that the child is helpless because of someone or something else. This sets a very tricky tone, giving all power away to an external person or circumstance and becoming reliant on something changing that you have no control over. On the other hand, dismissing a child's version of events can lead them to feel 'silly', and frustrated that nobody understands. This can then lead to a child repressing future negative feelings.

When a child reports an event negatively, it is important that a balance is struck, so the child feels heard and understood but also knows the positives they have contributed/can contribute as a 'take away' from the situation (positive Resilience). This balance can be achieved by using Empathic and Empowering language.

Imagine your child has had a disagreement with a friend at school. They come home with a grumpy face. The first thing to do is notice that they are in a bad mood. "You seem a little quiet, sweetheart." Note that this is an observation, not a question. When questioned, children feel under pressure or compelled to give you an answer they think you want to hear. When you make an observation, the child has more choice about whether they want to talk about how they are feeling in their own time. The child is also likely to feel that they are important, as the parent has noticed how they are showing their feelings while respecting that they may not want to talk about the situation. Your child is then likely to go on to tell you what has caused their mood. Let us imagine there was an incident with their friend at lunchtime, likely to be described as follows:

"It's that Joe. He is stupid. He told the teacher that I tripped him up when I didn't do anything. I hate him, and he is not my friend anymore."

An Empathic and Empowering response would be, "You seem really frustrated about that, and I can understand why. That was at lunchtime, so you must have shown really good <u>self-control</u>, <u>determination</u> and <u>problem-solving skills</u>, because Mrs N didn't call me over to talk to me. Well done for getting on with your day."

The conversation is unlikely to end there; the child is probably going to continue airing their grievances about their friend. Continue to use Empathic and Empowering language by empathising with how difficult it must have been to feel as the child felt then remind them of what skills they have that will help resolve the problem—not necessarily to make up with their friend, but to bring the situation to a satisfactory conclusion. You might get some under-the-breath mutterings and further complaints, but if you stay consistent with Empathic and Empowering language, your child will eventually cool down and soften their thoughts and feelings about the situation. As soon as this happens, an opportunity for Superpower language has arrived: "You were so angry earlier, but you have worked through it using your <u>communication</u>, <u>self-control</u> and <u>problem-solving skills</u>. I am really proud of you." With a younger child, you might say, "You were very cross, but you have told Mummy about it using your <u>talking to a grown-up</u> Superpower. You have <u>calmed down</u> now and seem much more <u>cheerful</u>, and I am really proud of you." This is another example of supportively challenging your child and promoting positive Resilience. The supportive part of this approach is that you have validated your child's feelings and reminded them of the skills they have shown and can show to continue to work through the problem. The challenge is that you have let them come around in their own time and draw their own conclusion without taking over or rescuing them. Using the Transformative Communication approaches suggested here, you have neither dismissed nor rescued them. This will help build a strong internal narrative: *My feelings are important, and I am listened to. I have skills that can get me through challenging situations.* If a child has something close to this as their internal narrative, they are likely to develop strong Resilience as they grow and mature.

vi) Responding to emotional crises

The use of language is slightly different here to the other examples in this list, as the parent needs to take a step-by-step approach to addressing an emotional crisis. Too much, too soon will not help the child who is in an emotional crisis. I will split 'emotional crises' into two examples: a child in crisis for what an adult sees as a 'good' reason, and a child in crisis for what an adult would consider a 'trivial' reason. We will start with an example of a child in an emotional crisis because their parent, who no longer lives with them, has failed to arrive for a planned visit. This is the third time in four weeks that this has happened. Let's imagine the child is inconsolable, sobbing and making incoherent noises. Initially, when a child is in such a state of crisis, they just need to know a parent is there. They will not be able to take in lots of dialogue, so a simple, "I can see how upset you are, sweetheart" will suffice to start with. It can be difficult for a parent to see their child in a distressed state, and there may be a temptation to 'fix' the problem (or rescue, as discussed in the previous example)—it is often a parent's instinct, and it can feel like 'just' empathising is not enough. However, I would encourage the parent to simply sit with the child and reiterate that they can see how distressed they are. The child's upset may turn to anger, saying things like, "I hate him", "He always does this!", "Am I not good enough for him?" and "I don't ever want to see him again!". It is important not to get into the content of what is said but focus on the emotion behind it—"I know you are really angry, and I understand why." As the child calms down, the parent can gently introduce some empowering language like, "You have been so <u>brave</u> since Dad left; so <u>adaptable</u> and so <u>Resilient</u>, just getting on with things. You've gone to school every day; you've not used it as an excuse. I am so proud of you." None of this changes the fact that the child feels let down, but it gives them a huge boost to know that they have already shown such positive skills to cope with such a difficult challenge. This Transformative Communication further highlights to the child that they have shown positive Resilience. As mentioned earlier in the chapter, the outcome hasn't changed, but the child has learnt something positive about themselves, and this will register as part of their inner voice. When the child calms down further, I would advise doing a nice activity with them and reiterating the strengths they have that will see them through this challenging situation.

Here, it is very tempting to 'rescue' your child and vent anger at the other parent who has let them down. However, this will only serve to build a negative narrative in the child. They will be unable to take control of how they feel, as they have the excuse of blaming someone else. While it is important to empathise with how the child is feeling, it is also important that the parent empowers the child to see how they can positively respond to the situation; otherwise the child becomes a victim of their circumstances. Support and rescue are very easy to confuse, particularly when a parent is feeling emotional themself. Second-guessing why another person (in the example used here, the child's dad) has acted in a seemingly inappropriate way is speculative and pointless. It is also difficult in these types of situations not to let your own thoughts and feelings cloud what you say about the other person. Focus on your child and how they are feeling. You and your child can do something about that. You cannot do anything about the actions of someone else, and it is only painful to try.

Moving on to an example of a child in crisis for a seemingly trivial reason, I will cover a common occurrence in younger children. When I work with parents of children between four and seven years old, it is not unusual to hear that the child overreacts to a seemingly small issue. A common theme is that a young child can be very particular about clothes, the shape/texture of their food, what they watch at a certain time and/or who takes them to bed. Empathic and Empowering language can cover any and all of this list of behaviours so they are nipped in the bud before they become a problem. No matter how trivial you believe the issue to be, look beyond the behaviour and focus on what your child is trying to tell you about how they are feeling—what is their inner voice saying? So, if they are sobbing and kicking the chair with snot all over their face, don't get into why it is ridiculous for them to respond like this because their cheese sandwich is cut into squares and not triangles; try to empathise with what they are feeling, then tell them what you want them to do to positively move forward: "Perhaps you are tired, hungry and fed up. I can see you are upset. I want you to try to <u>calm down</u>, and then we can sort this out." Then walk away calmly. You will tend to find, particularly with a younger child, that they feel better just knowing their parent knows how they feel. That is all they really needed. They will then be much more likely to eat the food, go to have their story with Dad, wear their black socks, or whatever they seemed so desperate to avoid!

vii) Responding to self-deprecating language

As I have mentioned, children will translate their inner beliefs through their behaviour. There are times, however, when a child is very explicit in the language they use to describe how they see themself. Many parents I work with report their child saying things such as, "I am stupid", "Nobody likes me", "Everybody hates me", "I always get everything wrong". In common with some of the other examples detailed in this chapter, it is very tempting to rescue and/or inadvertently dismiss your child in this situation. A natural and automatic response to "I am stupid" is "Of course you are not. Don't be silly!" Isn't silly another way of saying stupid? Parents respond in a way they think will help their child feel better, but dismissing their child's perception leads that child to feel unheard, invalidated and often worse than when they first ventured the self-deprecating language.

While I do not advocate a parent agreeing with a child's assertion that they are stupid, I recommend an Empathic and Empowering response, such as, "Really? Is that the way you feel? Stupid?" Wait for a reply, then add, "That must feel horrible, and I'm sorry you feel that way. What I see is a <u>cheerful</u>, <u>imaginative</u>, <u>independent</u> little girl with lots of energy and <u>enthusiasm</u>." I advise that you then wait to be led by your child. They will hopefully either seek comfort in the form of a hug or appear happier than before. If they want a hug, you know what to do! If they seem okay, redirect them to a different activity or leave them knowing they are okay.

The child's emotion scale

The series of scales on pages 56–59 illustrate how a child feels on a scale of 1–10 (10 being the most positive they can feel) throughout a challenging situation when a critical and judgemental adult intervenes.

Stage 1 – A child has an unmet need. They might not know what that need is, but they feel angry, anxious, frustrated, upset, etc.

10
9
8
7
6
5
4
3
2
1

Stage 2 – The child displays a survival behaviour that releases some of their negative energy; initially this release moves them up the scale.

10
9
8
7
6
5
4
3
2
1

Stage 3 – The child feels shame about what they have done. They may not show this outwardly, but they fall back down the scale.

10
9
8
7
6
5
4
3
2
1

Stage 4a – An adult intervenes, shouts at the child and criticises them. The child feels like nobody understands, and might blame, complain and/or get even more angry, as now they are in survival mode.

When a challenge escalates into a crisis as illustrated, it is as if the child has been left with a gaping wound, as they feel shame, self-loathing, anger and resentment—all of which are left unresolved. It is no surprise then that a child feeling these toxic emotions and thinking negatively will go on to display more poor behaviour, as they are trying to get even more unmet needs met. I often hear education professionals and parents say, "I knew what type of day we were in for the minute he walked through the door" and then describe how a child has lurched from one crisis to another. This is usually because the initial crisis wasn't resolved, and they are left with the debris of those feelings of shame, self-loathing, anger and resentment. I refer to this as 'day debris'. The day will only go one way if a child is carrying those toxic feelings around with them!

On to a more positive scenario. Below is an illustration of how a child goes through stages of a challenging situation when a supportive adult intervenes using Transformative Communication (NB Stages 1–3 are as already detailed).

Stage 4b – A supportive adult intervenes and empathises with how the child is feeling. This adds additional stages as the child moves out of the crisis.

10
9
8
7
6
5
4
3
2
1

Stage 5 – The adult talks to the child about the Superpowers they are already using and/or could use to try to resolve the problem.

Stage 6 – The supportive adult reminds the child of the Superpowers they can continue to use to ensure that the next part of their day is happier, adding evidence of a time the child has shown such Superpowers in previous situations. The child is calm, feels understood and heard and feels empowered to move forward.

The emotion scales illustrate the impact an adult can have through the language they use when a child is controlling a situation via their behaviour and/or showing negative emotions. The short-term (behaviour that day) and long-term (internal narrative) impact is dependent on the responses of the adult dealing with the child at the time they are facing a challenge. The two results are vastly different, dependent on which route you take.

How to add consequences without damaging Resilience/internal narrative

Parents sometimes ask if certain behaviours require a consequence and not 'just' Empathic and Empowering language. They understandably worry that, by not 'punishing' negative behaviour, they might be giving their child the impression that they can act and behave however they want. As we know, society has certain rules, and it is our job to prepare our children to be upstanding and law-abiding citizens. So, consequences are sometimes needed. It is how they are introduced and the language that is used in implementing them that is key to retaining the Resilience and positive internal narrative of your child.

If you notice a recurring behaviour that you want to change, there is a specific Transformative Communication technique to achieve change without shaming your child or damaging their internal narrative and Resilience. I call this a 'pre-conversation' or a 'reference-point conversation'. You have this conversation at a time when you and your child are calm—not in the middle of a crisis! Choosing a time to have the conversation is important, as you want your child to be receptive rather than defensive. A sensitive child will be easily upset, but the order of this conversation will hopefully alleviate this issue. Below is an example of a pre-conversation to address behaviour (the behaviour in this case being lashing out at a family member). Have the conversation in your child's room, with them on the bed and you on the floor (towering over them creates an immediate power imbalance and prepares the child for 'attack'). The conversation goes something like this:

1. ***Start with a positive to set the tone:*** This means your child is less likely to be defensive and switch off. Include Superpowers! "We have noticed you are showing <u>self-control</u> so much more than you used to. When you get cross, you often take yourself away from the situation. We are really proud of you. You're such a <u>caring</u> and <u>kind</u> boy."

2. *Notice the behaviour, but do not criticise it*: "We have noticed that you sometimes lash out and hit [name of person(s)]." No shaming needed, and then move on quickly to . . .

3. *Empathise with the 'why'*: "We wonder if this happens when you want to do something, and we say no. Sometimes maybe you are tired and hungry. We think that sometimes you might even be upset with yourself. We can see how frustrated you are when you lash out." If your child was about to go on the defensive after Point 2, this will bring them back to you.

4. *Tell the child what you DO want to see (as an alternative to the behaviour you described in Point 2), and invite them to come up with their own solution:* Use Superpower language. "When you start to feel angry, we want you to show your self-control to move away from [name of person(s)]. Then you can let out your anger in another way. What would help you to do that? What could you do to let your anger out safely?" By asking them what they think they can do, you are making this a collaborative effort. Your child feels, symbolically, that they can be part of the solution, not simply the problem (remember HK from earlier?). If they cannot come up with an alternative to let out their anger, offer some suggestions: a punch bag, an old pillow used specifically to let out anger on, shouting, etc. This lets your child know that it is okay to get angry. You are being realistic. Accepting that they are going to get angry is important. Anger is a much-maligned emotion, but one that everyone feels, and one that needs to be expressed. Anger itself is not a massive issue; inappropriate expression of anger is problematic. Using the collaborative approach suggested here gives your child some ownership of the issue and some choice. This is vital for a child, as when they 'think' they do not have a choice, they can use this as an excuse for negative behaviour.

5. *The consequence:* "If you do lash out, the consequence will be . . ." Think carefully here; you do not want to pick a consequence you either cannot stick to or causes you more

problems than it solves! Incremental consequences work well (i.e. "For every time you lash out, I will take five minutes away from ...").

This Transformative Communication approach includes a technique I call the 'positive sandwich'—Points 1 and 3 positively wrapping up the only slightly less positive Point 2. This technique can work well when trying to implement fair consequences, even if you have to think on your feet and don't have time for a reference-point conversation. For example, you are out, and your child behaves inappropriately when you really need them to comply. A positive sandwich would be, "You have been <u>cheerful</u> and <u>kind</u> this afternoon. I've had such a nice time with you. I know you don't want to get in the car and the journey is boring. I want you to <u>calm down</u> and get in the car. I am going to sort your brother out, and I trust you will be in your seat when I come back. If not, there will be no PS4 when we get home. Use your <u>self-control</u>, and sit in your seat. Thank you."

Using reference-point conversations and the positive-sandwich technique is a fair way of addressing behaviour while making your child aware of potential consequences. These techniques do not, however, guarantee that the behaviour will stop! Therefore, when the behaviour occurs, it is important to use Empathic and Empowering language again. Avoid language like, "I've tried doing it the nice the way. We sat down and had a calm conversation; but no, you just throw it back in my face" or, if your child cries or gets angry when you follow through with a consequence, "Well, it is your own fault. You've had plenty of warnings, and now the PS4 is going off for the night." This will undo the reference-point/positive-sandwich conversation. Instead, stick to, "I can see you are frustrated and upset that I have taken time on your PS4 away from you. I want you to try to <u>calm down</u>, and I'm going to trust you to do that <u>independently</u>." Then walk away. Having calm conversations with your child can help them understand that they need to change their behaviour without damaging their internal narrative. Introducing consequences combined with Empathic and Empowering language lets your child know that universally recognised inappropriate behaviour is not okay, but they retain your understanding and hear about Superpowers that they can use to take responsibility and positive ownership of such behaviour.

Missed opportunities vs. cementing learning

At times, all children, to varying degrees of severity, go through something tough. More often than not, the child comes through challenges, and this is highlighted when education professionals and parents say to me, "Kids are more Resilient than adults!" However, as I touched on earlier in the book, a child often does not know they have shown Resilience and certainly does not know how they have shown it. Unwittingly, we can teach children to develop survival Resilience—they got through a challenge but do not know how, and the child is simply relieved it is over. While this type of Resilience helps us go through a challenge, it rarely helps us *grow* through a challenge. In fact, a child's internal narrative can be damaged even though the perceived problem/challenge is over.

Achieving positive Resilience requires an adult to talk to the child about how they have used Superpowers to successfully navigate their way through a challenge. When this isn't done, opportunities to build a really strong internal narrative in a child are missed. Here I will give examples of how cementing a child's learning (positive Resilience) looks vs. missing an opportunity (survival Resilience), and the impact both scenarios can have.

I have picked a challenge that every child has recently gone through: coping with the changes enforced on children because of coronavirus. In trying to cope with 'Covid times', the scenario meant that children went through a lot of changes: they were either forced to stay off school, or they went to school in very different circumstances to usual as a child of a key worker. They couldn't go anywhere, couldn't see family or friends and had to do schoolwork at home. They were then told they could go back to school, but it would be very different to what they were used to and, dependent on their age, they could only go into school for one week before summer. After a short period, it was the summer holidays, and they were back at home before going back to school in September on a full-time basis after not being in a typical school environment for six months. In January 2021, schools closed to the majority of children again. Children have had to get used to adults wearing masks, waiting longer for medical/mental health appointments and clubs and sports that they loved being cancelled or indefinitely postponed. The scene is set. Let's look at how we can miss opportunities vs. achieving positive Resilience:

Missed opportunity: Feeling relieved that your child is back at school though saying nothing to them about how they have coped.

Approach: Whether the child had a good or bad experience of lockdown/Covid times and all the changes described above, you are simply happy that it is over and assume they are too. You make no mention of the Superpowers they have shown during these times.

Short-term impact: Children learn nothing about the skills they showed to either get through the challenge or to make it okay for themselves. Their mentality will either be, *I didn't like being at home all that time. Lockdown was rubbish. I'm glad it is over* or *Lockdown wasn't that bad.* Note the black-and-white thinking of a child! They are putting all the emphasis on external circumstances and factors and cannot see how they impacted on the situation at all.

Long-term impact: When an everyday challenge comes up, they don't know which skills they drew on during a global crisis, and so treat this more trivial challenge as if it is just as severe. They have learnt nothing about themselves.

Cementing your child's learning: Employing Transformative Communication to make a beneficial impact upon the internal narrative of the child.

Approach: Whether your child experienced lockdown/Covid times as negative, positive or a little of both, tell them about the Superpowers you noticed that they showed throughout: adaptability, Resilience, resourcefulness, independence, imagination, creativity, problem-solving skills, self-entertaining, self-control, determination and diligence in the following of instructions. You encourage your child to look at how they can transfer these skills to other potentially challenging situations, big or small.

Short-term impact: The child now knows how they positively took control of a situation that they neither asked for nor wanted. They know they were not reliant on external circumstances for them to be okay, as they have Superpowers that helped them cope, whatever the outcome. Children become aware that they have shown positive Resilience.

Long-term impact: The child has a significant reference point that they can look to as evidence that their skills outweigh challenges that are out of their control. By reminding them of the Superpowers they have shown during the crisis, you are cementing their learning, and they are likely to be more sustainably Resilient. Your child will know that, should another challenge come along, they have transferable tools to deal with anything. They feel powerful, strong and confident. Your child starts to see that the skills they showed during the crisis are transferable to many different situations.

As with the two examples of adult responses and the impact they have on a child's emotions scale, the use of Transformative Communication in this scenario can make a huge short- and long-term difference to your child's internal narrative. Challenges present opportunities. We just have to look for them.

Making sure Empathy and Empowering language works

The following three Transformative Communication tips can help you make sure that your Empathic and Empowering language works well:

- Say 'thank you', not 'please'. Saying 'thank you' before a child has complied with something you have suggested implies, in a positive way, that you expect them to complete the action.
- Use 'perhaps' and 'I'm wondering if ...' when you are empathising. Sometimes 'telling' a child how they are feeling might antagonise them further. 'Pondering language' is gentler and gives them the chance to tell you if you have guessed wrongly about how they are feeling.
- Tell your child what you *do* want; do not criticise what you *don't* like. It is so easy to say things like, "I have told you I don't know how many times about this. You just don't listen, do you?" A much more positive way to address a behaviour is, "I'm wondering if you are still upset about coming off your game. I want you to listen to me for a moment. Thank you." Then set an expectation of what you want, and include Superpower language, so that the child knows they have the power to achieve the expectation you have set.

Damage and repair

During my postgraduate Psychotherapy and Counselling course, we participated in 'personal development', where all eleven members of the course sat in a circle and tried to discuss the impact that people within the circle had on each other. As you can imagine, this was awkward and certainly did not feel natural. While it was easy to tell someone they had a *positive* impact on me, I found it incredibly unnatural to speak openly and honestly about someone having a *negative* impact on me. Richard Davis, course leader and one of the most inspiring men I have come across, took me to one side one week and asked, "Nick, when you were younger, were you allowed to destroy things?"

Taken aback, I stuttered, "Wh-what do you mean?"

Richard elaborated, "If you broke or destroyed something, what happened?"

I said, "Whatever it was I'd broken would be taken away from me, and I'd have to wait for a birthday or Christmas to replace it. And I got shouted at."

"You can tell," Richard said. "You don't know how to destroy someone because you are fearful you will not be able to repair that relationship." He went on to say that in regular lectures I was a vocal and interactive member of the course—never afraid to give my thoughts. However, in personal development, when there was a danger that my words might upset someone, I remained quiet. This was true, and I was flabbergasted that Richard had known I wasn't allowed to destroy things when I was younger simply from observing me in a group. This insight highlights the importance of damage and repair for children. If a child is simply punished for damaging something, they cannot be part of the resolution of the problem. As with me, this can infiltrate areas of their life as they grow. So, if your child damages something—even it seems beyond repair—it is crucial that they get the chance to try to repair the object, with your help if needed.

Summary

I am aware that this is the longest chapter in the book; I've given you a lot to process! In summary, use of the Empathic and Empowering language in the various ways I have detailed in this chapter will lead to positive cycles, even in challenging situations. Consistent positive cycles will lead to a sustainable change in your child's internal narrative and Resilience. The positive cycles start with Superpower language—as detailed in the previous chapter—and it is essential that this is present for Empathic and Empowering language to work. I encourage parents to get into the mindset of seeing opportunity in challenge. We only know we have Resilience when something tough occurs, so don't fight challenges and wish they didn't happen—they will happen anyway! And when those challenges come along, in using the language I have illustrated in this chapter, you will create an opportunity for your child to learn something positive about themselves and develop positive Resilience. I call this a 'win-win' mentality—negative and challenging situations are never a waste of time if you and your child learn something positive from such moments. In fact, that is precisely how positive Resilience is formed and how people develop.

How a child views themself in difficult times is crucial as to whether they take positive learning about themselves from challenges or simply continue to self-loath, blame, resent and avoid. Coasting along peacefully sounds great, and it is necessary for periods of time. However, we don't learn a lot about ourselves or our children when things are going swimmingly. Just enjoy those moments, always mindful that when a challenge arises, you can deal with it positively. I saw on an inspiring quotes video recently that 'the difference between an ordeal and an adventure is attitude'. So, we can get stressed and think negatively about our child's behaviour, or we can accept it, supportively challenge it and move forward positively. There is much more on how to free yourself up to do this in the next chapters. Establishing more positive cycles leads to a child believing they are strong, independent, a problem-solver, Resilient and resourceful in the face of challenges. A child with this view of themself will be much more likely to have good relationships, make good lifestyle choices, have high expectations, model appropriate behaviour and offer something special to the world.

Case study: The hole in my pants!

PK was an adopted child I worked with from the age of seven to
ten. He was adopted aged four, had no language when he arrived
with his adopted family and was emotionally, socially and
academically behind his peers when I first started my work with
him and his family. I worked extensively with PK, his adoptive
parents and the education professionals involved. Much of what I
promoted was linked to looking beyond his behaviour and
focussing on what was driving it (the inner voice). This was
particularly difficult for all involved, as PK's behaviour was
extreme and difficult to manage. He was quite obstructive in our
one-to-one sessions; he would display many of the classic
behaviours I described in Chapter 2: lying, not engaging, avoiding
tasks and criticising his peers, siblings and teachers. There were
times when, after a whole lot of Empathy and Empowerment, I felt
it best to positively cut the session short, as I didn't think he was
gaining anything from it.

On one cold November morning we sat in the space where we
had our session. Space is at a premium in schools, so I go where I
am told to go (within reason!). The after-school team used the
room where PK and I had our sessions. This meant that a whole
plethora of goodies were close by: glue sticks, rulers, crayons and
... scissors. PK got out of his seat as we were talking. As always, I
verbally observed his body language and gave him some time to
decide what to do next. PK picked up some scissors. I
acknowledged this and reminded him that the scissors belonged to
the after-school club and asked him to put them down. PK took his
trousers, just above the knee, gathered a bit of fabric and cut a
significantly sized hole. He then put the scissors down, and we
carried on with the session. After our session I told the teacher
what had happened and encouraged her not to draw too much
attention to the hole in PK's pants. I then rang PK's adoptive dad

to explain what had happened and advise him on how to handle it in keeping with the approach we had been using thus far. PK's dad's initial reaction was exasperation—"It is always something with him!"

I let him vent then asked, "How are you going to handle this when he gets home?"

Dad informed me that he would let PK know that money for trousers is hard earned, that he needs to learn value for money and that there would be a consequence for his actions. Thinking about damage and repair and the wise words of Richard Davis, I encouraged dad to take a different route. "Do you have a sewing kit?" I asked.

"I think so," Dad replied hesitantly.

"Okay. When PK gets back, acknowledge the hole but do not criticise him. Keep it factual. Don't give him a reason to get his defences up. Encourage him to go with you and your wife to the sewing kit, and let him play a part in the repair of the pants. Even if you put a square patch over the hole and sew it on, let him see that the pants can be repaired." dad reluctantly agreed to give this a try, and I reminded him to back it up with Empathic and Empowering language. I left dad with a warning: "If this works, PK has to wear the pants to school at least once, so he knows you are not just humouring him!"

A week later I received a call from PK's dad. What followed was a conversation that is still one of the highlights of my working life. PK's dad and I exchanged pleasantries before I enquired, "So, how did it go last week?"

"That is what I am ringing for actually. He came in looking very guilty, we did what you said and he sat by the sewing kit not knowing what to do or say. I told him that he could use his keen eye to pick some fabric that might match his pants, and he did. I told him I trusted him to hold the fabric in place while Mum went around it with a needle and thread. He smiled. He chatted to us about his day. He has never done that! We sat like a family on a postcard, had a hot chocolate and repaired his pants. I said to him that I didn't know why he had cut a hole in his pants but empathised with the urge he must have had to do it and encouraged him to use <u>self-control</u> if he felt this urge again. He went to bed at 8 p.m., asked for an extra story and told me and my wife 'I love you' as we left the room."

Delighted and emotional, I gathered myself before asking, "Previously, when he has done something he perceives to be wrong at school, what normally happens?"

Dad said, "We are stern with him, and he gets very angry, tells us he hates us, slams doors, trashes his room and becomes hysterical. Often we forget what the original reason for the upset was, as by 10 p.m. we are all exhausted, and he cries himself to sleep."

This helped dad to see the extraordinary difference that Transformative Communication and a thought-out approach can have.

I will never forget dad's next words: "We cannot tell you what a difference this has made to us. That evening is the best we've had with him since he came to live here. We felt 'connected' with him, and it has given us so much hope and confidence moving forward." As this wonderful phone call drew to a close, dad hit me with a warning tone. "I have something to discuss with you before you go. You have made one thing very difficult for us."

Worried, I stuttered, "Oh? W-what is it?"

He then said, "These ******* pants are his favourite thing in the world, and we have to send him to school in them every day!"

There is a very happy ending to this story. PK is now a teenager and attending college every day. He has ambitions to go on to work as a mechanic. While still behind academically, PK manages his emotions well and has a solid group of good friends. He is popular, independent and a credit to his adoptive parents. He has moments of angst, like any teenager, but compared to the worries his adoptive parents had, the issues he presents with are minimal.

PK has developed Resilience as he has grown and matured; this is down, in no small part, to the collective effort of his adoptive parents and the education professionals who have worked with him along the way.

When PK was eight years old, he had a teacher who proved to be pivotal to his amazing turnaround. This teacher's enthusiasm to take on the Transformative Communication approaches suggested in this book knew no bounds. PK's behaviour often distracted the whole class, making her job of teaching thirty children extremely difficult. During one lesson that I happened to be observing, the teacher used Transformative Communication in the form of Empathy and Empowerment in a way that I still reference as the benchmark for teachers to aim towards. An angry PK came into class late after lunch, throwing a football against the wall near where he sat. The teacher was in the middle of teaching a handwriting lesson. She slowly signalled to the class to be patient for a moment, sat at a nearby desk and said quietly, "I see you are angry. It is difficult to come back into class and focus when something is clearly upsetting you so much. I understand." As the teacher spoke, PK's body language changed significantly: the velocity of his throws of the football reduced, his face softened and his shoulders went from taught and tense to relaxed and dropped. The teacher added, "I have seen you show great focus, self-control, determination and problem-solving skills this week. Keep that in mind for this afternoon." Then gave PK a friendly smile and carried on teaching. After a few moments, PK stopped throwing the ball and leaned against the wall near his desk. The teacher made a deliberate mistake on the board to challenge the children's keen eyes. As many of the class were shouting joyously to highlight the teacher's mistake, I looked at PK, and he too was shouting enthusiastically. To be so engaged so quickly after feeling so angry was incredible, mainly thanks to some inspired Transformative Communication from a brave teacher who was willing to put the language to the test, even in extremely challenging circumstances. All teachers have targets to reach and are expected to help ALL children fulfil their potential. So, when one child causes the disruption PK was causing, it would be easy to hold negative thoughts and feelings towards that child and simply make that child the responsibility of someone else: the teaching assistant, extra learning support, the deputy head teacher or the head teacher. This teacher, however, was so committed to making a positive difference to PK's life and was able to look beyond his behaviour. He flourished while with her, and her understanding, nurturing and Empathic and Empowering approach played a significant part in changing PK's internal narrative. From there, he has never looked back.

CHAPTER 5

Should've, Could've, Would've

When a child displays negative behaviour, appears consistently unhappy and/or seems constantly anxious, it is wearing on the adults around that child. No matter how much you love your child and want them to be happy, their actions are at odds with what you need to do, how you want to feel and how you wish you could see them. It is not unusual for me to hear parents saying, "Why does it have to be *my* child who behaves that way? Why can they not just get on with it and be happy like their friends?" This type of 'why me?' thinking, while understandable, only serves to cause greater frustration to the person thinking those thoughts. Such thoughts tend to lead to 'if only' and 'should/shouldn't' thinking; but this is a fantasy—a figment of the imagination—and when everyday life proves that this fantasy is not real, the frustration levels get higher and higher and higher! Holding frustration that is connected to your child will make it more difficult for you to put in place the Transformative Communication strategies suggested so far. So, in this chapter I will highlight the perils of 'should' and 'shouldn't' thinking and suggest some techniques to adapt these thoughts. I hope that by the end of this book you will be able to think, *Why me? Why not?* and find the peace that comes with this thinking.

The perils of 'should and shouldn't' thinking

The four brief statements that follow illustrate examples of 'should and shouldn't' thinking, something that the vast majority of people will do without realising they are doing it.

"He *should* be able to do that by now."

"She *shouldn't* still be doing that at her age."

"He *should* be able to deal with that without having a meltdown."

"She *shouldn't* be lashing out."

We see a behaviour we don't like and create an alternate universe in our minds where this behaviour doesn't happen. We then think that this version of reality is what 'should' be happening. The issue here is this: whatever the behaviour you don't like is, it is happening and whatever you think your child 'should' be able to do, they are not doing it. By thinking 'should' and 'shouldn't', you are fighting reality. Let me give you a couple of examples.

Child H is slamming doors, talking back at his mum and not complying very often when she asks him to do something. Mum says to me, "He shouldn't be slamming doors."

I say, "But is he slamming doors?"

Mum laughs, "Well, yes."

I add, "So, let's deal with the fact he is slamming doors rather than fantasise about him not doing it." Keep in mind that I have a good and established rapport with the parent in question; I might change the tone if I don't know the parent, but the message is the same!

Another, slightly different, example will illustrate the point further. Child Y gets extremely anxious about going to school. He has friends, achieves well academically and his teacher always reports that he calms down quickly once the school day has started. Mum says to me, "He shouldn't be crying like this in the mornings. He is ten years old."

I reply by saying, "But is he crying in the mornings?"

Mum answers with, "Yes, but he is ten."

I continue by saying, "He is ten years old, and he is crying in the morning. Take away what you think *should* be happening and let us treat this as a fact. He is ten and he is crying—we think because he is anxious in the mornings?"

Mum confirms that with a "Yes".

I then challenge her by saying, "Okay. So what shall we do about it?" I go on to remind her about using Superpower language, which has slipped in the case of this parent, and re-establishing Empathic and Empowering language.

So why do we think 'should' and 'shouldn't' thoughts if they only cause frustration? Byron Katie wrote a fabulous book entitled *Loving What Is* (2002). Katie discusses at length how we add 'our story' onto situations. This ties in nicely with what I have written regarding internal narratives. It is not just children who have internal narratives; we all have them. By the time we have become adults, our internal narratives have had time to become so established that we may develop uninvestigated, throw-away thoughts and statements that are unwittingly driven by the story we tell ourselves and, indeed, have told ourselves for many years. It is natural, then, that our internal narrative (or story) governs the way we react to any situation—including how we react to our children. While Katie's book is not about parenting, so many of her concepts can be applied to how we deal with children. So, if a person heard a lot of unexpected shouting, saw violence and felt distressed by this in their childhood, part of their story is 'shouting and violence is bad'. When that person becomes a parent of more than one child and inevitably hears raucous shouting and sees pushing, shoving and hitting, their story goes with them—'shouting and violence is bad'. They perceive typical sibling aggression as 'violence', because they are sensitive to this type of behaviour. The story the parent attaches to the behaviour can develop further—*I 'shouldn't' be hearing and seeing this after what I have gone through*. Specific behaviours can bring something up in that parent, and they react accordingly. Alternatively, someone else might have grown up with lots of siblings of a similar age and loved the rough and tumble of fighting and shouting with their brothers and sisters. They look back on their childhood fondly. So, when they become a parent and hear lots of shouting and see lots of rough and tumble, they smile and remember the good days with their siblings. The stories that two different people attach to the same behaviour will dictate how they react to that behaviour.

Acceptance: the key to peace, not the excuser of awful behaviour!

There is a big difference between accepting that a behaviour is happening and excusing that behaviour. Parents I have worked with do not want to fall into the category of excusing their child's behaviour and, at times, overreact to that behaviour to try to stop it. As illustrated by examples within the book so far, overreaction only serves to perpetuate the behaviour rather than alleviate it. Positive acceptance of a behaviour means that we acknowledge that a certain behaviour is happening, that we want to do something about it and that we have the tools to positively challenge this behaviour (as the previous chapters have shown you). What we *don't* need is the stress, anxiety, anger, fear, guilt and resentment that a parent can feel when their child displays negative behaviour. So, acceptance does not involve thinking, *He punched his brother in the face. That is fine. Let me find the sweets for him!* Acceptance would involve thinking along the lines of, *He has punched his brother in the face. I will challenge this appropriately, deal with it and come to a positive conclusion.*

By the way, it is absolutely justifiable for a parent to be upset if they see their child hit another person! However, like with any shock, the parent needs to move on positively in order to effectively challenge the behaviour. Only try to move on and address behaviours such as this when you are ready. Byron Katie has a useful strategy to help someone move on from automatic negative thinking. Here, I will relate the strategy to a parent who, when addressing their child slamming doors and kicking walls, is struggling to leave behind her own attached stories and judgements. Katie encourages us to take a step back when we have an automatic negative thought like, *They shouldn't be doing that* and ask ourselves, *Is that categorically true?* We might not want our child to be doing that, but the truth is, they are doing that. Next, Katie prompts us to ask ourselves, *What do I think and feel, and how do I act when I* do *allow myself to think, 'They shouldn't be doing that?'* Normally, the answer to that question is a sequence of negative thoughts, feelings and actions. Finally, Katie invites people to consider, *How would it be for me if I looked at this situation without my story? If my story didn't exist? If I looked at this situation neutrally?* This requires some time and a little imagination. For a parent trying this technique, I encourage them to try to visualise this different way of thinking—if only for a moment or two. This creates a different picture in the parent's mind and gives them an alternative way at looking at their child's behaviour. The case study at the end of this chapter perfectly illustrates how this technique can transform a parent's approach with their child.

Judgement is useful in many ways. If we see a bus coming down the road at 40 mph, we hold our child's hand tighter and remind them that we wait until the bus goes past before we cross. If a tree is swinging wildly in the wind, we might cross over to the other pavement. If a small child is approaching a lit fire, we safely move them away. We notice the boss is in a terrible mood, so we know that today is not the day to ask for a pay rise! Judgement and 'our story' serve us so well and are critical to our survival. However, it can cause problematic issues when dealing with the behaviour of our children and in relation to how we think about our children. When we remove our judgement/'our story' that we attach to behaviour, or how our child is in general, it frees us up to calmly deal with the child in a more neutral way. In summary, if you find yourself saying and thinking 'should' and 'shouldn't', look at what is happening. If what is happening is positive, use Superpower language. If what is happening is negative, use Empathic and Empowering language. Use this as a rule of thumb. Put your energy into this, and you will see results. Energy spent thinking about what 'should' and 'shouldn't' be is wasted energy, and I for one know that parents do not have a lot of surplus energy to waste!

Case study: The day I stopped saying 'should', and the peace I have found since

This case study is slightly unusual, as the subject of the case study is ... me! More specifically, the flawed thinking I allowed myself to get into with my eldest son, who, for his privacy, I will refer to as AF. As I mentioned in Chapter 1, I have four children, and although I consider it my purpose as well as my career to help improve Resilience in children, I am only human and sometimes get exasperated with my own kids. Around the time I read the aforementioned *Loving What Is* (2002) by Byron Katie, my then eight-year-old was going through a stage of showing what is commonly known as a 'bad attitude'. He was aggressively shouting, complaining about his life, being rude to my wife and being very negative towards his younger siblings. Busy with my career, a new baby and self-development, I found myself using language like, "You are bored? When I was younger, I had to entertain myself in the holidays. Get on with it and stop moaning" or "You are so ungrateful" or "Stop being so negative towards your brothers" (the irony!) or "How dare you speak to your mummy like that. Get to your room"—no Empathic or Empowering language there. Looking at that list of statements makes me shudder; my only saving grace was that I realised the pattern I was getting into and was determined to amend it.

Doing what I do, theoretically and intellectually, I knew precisely the approach I needed to take: to use Superpower language when AF was doing okay and Empathic and Empowering language when he showed challenging behaviour, complained or appeared unhappy. I made and displayed a visual representation of AF's skills on the fridge and spoke to him about expecting to hear more language about his Superpowers from Mummy and Daddy. I was also armed with my knowledge of Empathic and Empowering language. For a few days, peace descended on the Dux household. I was more mindful of talking to AF about his Superpowers and tried to look beyond his behaviour when he did shout, complain, blame and/or lash out—intellectually and theoretically simple, though emotional matters are a bit more complex. My intellectual, thought-out, prepared responses had changed; however, my instinctive thoughts hadn't. Even through my false smile, I still found myself thinking, *He should be more grateful, He shouldn't be complaining. What does he have to complain about?, He shouldn't be so loud and aggressive, He should know by now to be a bit more patient with his younger brothers.* These thoughts can be summed up by a basic belief that I had developed—*He shouldn't be like he is*—fed by a deeper issue related to 'my story' and an even more damaging belief: *You've got it so much better than I did, and it is still not enough.* At its heart, this belief was almost completely driven by 'my story' rather than having much to do with my son. This concoction of negativity led to feelings of invisible, but damaging, resentment. AF was basically not living up to 'my story' that I had written for him. He didn't even know it existed, the poor boy.

Luckily, as I mentioned, I was reading *Loving What Is* around the time that the above was happening. I thought, *I need to apply this to my thinking about AF*, so I picked one of my thoughts—*He shouldn't be complaining*—and asked myself, *Is this categorically true?* Firstly, it is up to him if he wants to complain, so if he thinks he should complain, then who am I to tell him he can't? Secondly, he was an eight-year-old boy who had just had a baby sister (the first girl in a family of three boys. You can only imagine!). His nana was terminally ill, his friends played for longer on their consoles than him, and his little brothers, in his mind, were constantly annoying him. When I took a step back, he had a lot to complain about! I realised that one of my irritations was that I didn't want him to be a 'complainer'. I wanted him to be grateful, to see the positives in situations and to be Resilient. It occurred to me that what I hated so much about AF's behaviour was that he was acting like a 'victim', and I realised that one of my own biggest fears is becoming a 'victim'—my story was hugely impacting on my thoughts and feelings towards AF. These core beliefs I had in my own internal narrative were leading me to think that AF 'should' and 'shouldn't' behave in certain ways.

On to that damaging narrative—*You've got it so much better than I did, and it is still not enough.* I work hard as a parent to help give my children a happy, well-balanced life. Isn't it ironic, then, that I resented the fact that AF had such a life? I went through all of my 'should' and 'shouldn't' thoughts and asked myself, *Is that categorically true?* Each time, I arrived at another core belief I had that was driving my negative thinking. AF was not doing anything wrong; he was being a little boy. My inner 'little boy' could not handle that! I also realised that AF was mirroring how I spoke to him in the way he spoke to his little brothers. These realisations led me to positively change my communication with him. I must confess, I still get frustrated with AF's behaviour, but this is an initial reaction rather than a long-standing, resentful frustration. Whenever I catch myself reacting in a frustrated way with AF, I don't beat myself up, otherwise I am in another 'shouldn't' trap—*I shouldn't get frustrated!* I accept I am feeling frustrated, and I ask myself what 'should' or 'shouldn't' type of thinking I am allowing to govern my thoughts about AF ... and I always find one. This has really helped me to move on from situations much quicker and has certainly transformed my ability to let go of the negative thoughts and feelings that were starting to damage my relationship with AF. I can sometimes feel unhappy, as this type of self-reflection can uncover another part of 'my story' that I might need to deal with, but at least I am not unhappy with my son.

I have tried to stop saying 'should' and 'shouldn't' completely, replacing those words with, "I would like it if . . ." or "I think you can . . .", and then referencing Superpowers that AF has to help him achieve the expectation I have set. If he chooses not to follow my lead, I empathise with why and empower him again. I now know, emotionally and practically (not just intellectually), how to make the biggest impact in AF's life. I love AF, I am connected with him, I would do anything for him and I am proud of him. Whatever the 'thing' is that you have with a child, it is there. I look at him sometimes, and tears fill my eyes for no other reason than the fact that he is my son. I have always felt like that about him. Even with that foundation, 'should' and 'shouldn't' thinking and my 'stories' were ruining our relationship. Finding the key to challenging my thoughts has opened me up to use the Transformative Communication I so passionately believe in and have detailed in this book. I include my own experience not as a moment of self-indulgence in the book, but because I think a lot of the readers may have the intention of using the strategies but be held back by their own 'should' and 'shouldn't' thinking—their own 'story'. I hope this helps you know that you can change those thoughts.

CHAPTER 6

State Changers

You will have days when you are tired, stressed and don't feel like being positive with your child. You may also doubt yourself, be frustrated with yourself and feel anxious. It is at times like these that you will need to change your 'state'. Your ability to do this will determine whether or not you can put in place the Transformative Communication suggested in previous chapters. We often think of 'state' as a bad thing—"They were in a real state." However, we are going to focus on uplifting your state, as a positive state is key to being able to consistently use Transformative Communication that will make the biggest impact on your children. In *The Leader's Guide to Presenting*, Tom Bird and Jeremy Cassell discuss the importance of a person's state when trying to lead an individual or team in a positive change—exactly what this book aims to help you do with your child(ren). They define 'state' as 'a combination of beliefs, emotions, thoughts and physiology' (Bird and Cassell, 2017), so I will introduce a series of activities that can help transform those elements of yourself onto a sustainably positive plain.

The Book of Positivity

The 'Book of Positivity' is basically a positive daily diary. This can be kept in note form on your phone, tablet, laptop or in the traditional form of a diary that you can write in. Each day look for positive conversations, things that made you smile, a nice view, a compliment you received, a difference you made to someone, a time when you reacted positively to a challenge and, thinking about the content of this book, an incident when your child did something positive and/or times when you used Transformative Communication. Look for anything that was positive in your day. You may have the opportunity to make entries as they happen or have small moments of reflection time to note positives, or you can look back at your day retrospectively—compartmentalising your day into smaller sections is crucial for this to work. While, of course, I would recommend you include groundbreaking and major positive events, do not wait for such events before writing in your diary—not all of the entries have to be examples of huge positives. A number of small positives noted down in diary form will help cement the fact that much more good stuff is happening in your life than you perhaps realise.

As I discussed in Chapter 3, we tend to operate in a society that has a negativity bias—negatives come easily! Remember my description of my day to my wife? Committing to a positive diary trains our brains to look for positives. Writing/noting them down helps you remember those positives and creates a more even balance between positive and negative, countering the negativity bias. I have worked with people who, perhaps sceptical of change, have only half-committed to this concept. To use a real-life example but protect the person's privacy, Lady A once said to me, "I am starting to look for positives, but I'm not writing them down." She then told me about an example from the previous week, when she noticed a positive she normally wouldn't have acknowledged. A good start, but that is one example out of 119 waking hours! When I challenged Lady A to name five positive things that happened the previous day, she struggled to name just two. In writing your positives in diary form, you are making a commitment that you are likely to persevere with. In my experience, when people decide to think positively without making a commitment like a positive diary, this way of thinking is inconsistent and does not last. By committing to a positive diary, you can also look back to remind yourself of the positives you enjoy each day.

I mentioned earlier on in the book that I have been through anxiety and panic attacks. At the peak of an anxious period in 2007, I sought the help of a cognitive behaviour therapist. A simple thing he said to me about recognising positivity stayed with me. He likened our minds to filing cabinets: one drawer for positives and one for negatives. It is amazing how quickly the negative drawer fills up with minor, everyday irritations. However, we tend to be ignorant to the minor positives that are around us and within us all day, every day. A balance must be struck, and we have to consciously work at seeing positives, as unfortunately we recognise negatives subconsciously, and consciously and store them automatically.

Going back to Lady A, during a morning appointment I had with her she looked particularly flustered. I verbally noted this, and she said, "It has been one of those mornings. I spilt my cup of tea all over my shirt, and I had to change." (As an aside, do you notice that a negative set of events gets its own stock phrase—"One of those mornings"? Do we have one for when things go well?) I smiled and asked, "So, did you store that in your negativity file?" (She knew what this meant, as I had spoken to her about the filing cabinet analogy).

Laughing, Lady A replied, "Yes, I suppose I did!"

I then asked, "Okay. So tomorrow morning let's imagine you have one of those cups of tea that is just right; it is lovely, and you don't spill it! Do you store that in your positive file?"

Lady A laughed again and said, "I realise that I would be in such a rush, the nice tea wouldn't register."

So, we can be in too much of a rush to enjoy something, but we are never in too much of a rush to complain about something! Actions have to be taken to rectify this, or these seemingly trivial, everyday negatives start to stack up, and before too long our negativity cabinet is full and our positive cabinet looks sparse. Remember the 'positivity radar' from Chapter 3? The positive diary can help you hone this radar, as you are actively looking for positives that you might otherwise have missed. There is a famous old story of a Cherokee grandfather teaching his grandson about life. He talks about having a 'bad wolf' and a 'good wolf' within us. The 'bad wolf' is represented by anger, envy, sorrow, regret, greed, arrogance, self-pity, guilt, resentment, inferiority, lies, false pride, superiority and ego. The 'good wolf' is our joy, hope, peace, love, serenity, humility, kindness, benevolence, empathy, generosity, truth, compassion and faith. The little boy asks, "Which wolf will win?"

The grandfather replies, "The one you feed."

Feeding our 'good wolf' with positivity is essential to keep the 'bad wolf' at bay.

Developing an 'attitude of gratitude'

Jack Canfield, author of *The Success Principles* (2004) and the *Chicken Soup for the Soul* series, coined the phrase 'attitude of gratitude'. Jack encourages people to take a moment in their day to remind themselves of the things for which they are grateful. Jack talks about being grateful for the simple things in life; as with the Book of Positivity, you don't have to find monumental or life-changing things to be grateful for—although it is fantastic if you can. I have heard people say, "You either feel grateful or you don't. You can't force yourself to feel gratitude." While it is not possible to force gratitude, it is possible to practise thinking grateful thoughts and getting your mind more used to looking for things to be thankful for. Your mind is like a muscle and needs to be used in different ways to keep developing. Repetition of thoughts can condition your mind to create new pathways aligned with the new thoughts. So, practising gratitude will make you more grateful!

Tony Robbins, author and motivational life coach, professes that it is impossible to feel fear, anxiety, resentment and anger when we feel true gratitude. At times, thinking of something positive and/or something that we are grateful for is the last thing on our mind. I am aware that sometimes people 'need' to be grumpy for a while. However, having a tactic (or state changer) in your locker that will bring you out of this mood is important, as you can then free yourself up to be positive with your child once more. You will find that the

Book of Positivity compliments the 'attitude of gratitude', as it will help you see life's blessings and, in turn, help in the development of an 'attitude of gratitude'. Remember at the start of the chapter I mentioned that 'state' was made up of beliefs, emotions, thoughts and physiology? Using the Book of Positivity and an 'attitude of gratitude' can help you *think* differently, and, in turn, you can *feel* differently (emotions). This can help you in the formation of new and more positive beliefs. Believe it or not, having more positive beliefs about yourself has an impact on your physiology too. Gratitude plays a part in this. Dr Joe Dispenza, a neuroscientist and author, references evidence that gratitude improves health, particularly your heart health. I recommend any of his books if you wish to learn more about this.

Affirmations

I first got the idea of using positive affirmations from *Feel the Fear and Do It Anyway* (1987) by Susan Jeffers. I emphatically recommend this book. Reading it completely changed my life. Known as *'Feel The Fear'* for short, I credit this book for setting me on the path to being self-employed, reducing anxiety, improving some damaged relationships and helping me find my true calling in life. One of the staple exercises in the book is the use of positive affirmations. Affirmations are basically positive statements said in the present tense. So, in this context, I want you to draw up a list of positive statements about yourself and your life. Do not worry if your list is short to start with; you will add to it as you go along. Think about what you have achieved in your life: your family, your job, your relationships, overcoming challenges, owning/renting a house, the difference you make to the world, and your hobbies. Hopefully, you will be able to pick out some strengths you needed along the way to achieve your current standing in life. Sometimes, looking at your Book of Positivity will inform your list of affirmations. Remember, you don't have to be a multi-millionaire, a champion athlete or a Nobel Peace Prize winner to have achieved success. Success is relative to your situation, so give yourself a break and really take the time to appreciate your strengths and blessings. Even if you are feeling down, look hard enough, and you will see some of your strengths. An example list may look like this:

I write my own narrative;

I am Resilient;

I am resourceful;

I am loving;

I have the strength to overcome setbacks;

I am free.

When you have established your list, move on to saying these statements out loud—if possible, in front of a mirror! You are essentially telling yourself that you have these skills, blessings, opportunities or whatever the affirming statement represents. If this feels uncomfortable, it is just your inner negative voice trying to keep you locked in negativity. It is easy to be conditioned to think that ideas like this are 'silly'. With time you will be able to do this. At the other side of discomfort is growth and progress.

Once you have spent some time (a couple of weeks) practising saying your statements in the mirror, try to add in the 'feeling' of the statements. Try imagining how you would act, how people would respond to you, which barriers would be removed, what opportunities would open up and how you would feel about yourself if you truly believed and felt every affirming statement. Really live the statement as if it were 100 per cent true. Picture yourself living the affirmation. By feeling these statements, you are adding an emotional 'truth' to them. Reading the statements tells your mind that they could be true, and hearing them makes them truer. Reading, hearing and seeing someone (you) saying the statements makes them seem even truer still. Reading, hearing, seeing and feeling the statements on repeat gives all-round positive messages and imagery to your subconscious mind about yourself. You are writing your own internal narrative.

Why are affirmations important?

I have referred to negativity bias several times in this book. Unfortunately, we do not often hear positive things about ourselves from other people—if we wait for external praise, we could be waiting a long time! We do, however, hear or perceive criticism on a regular basis and subsequently self-criticise to compound criticism from others. Les Brown quotes an MIT University study that found that if we hear "*You can't do it*" once, we need to hear "You *can* do it" sixteen times before we believe it to be true! Using affirmations is a way of taking proactive action and not waiting for someone else's 'permission' to feel good about ourselves. In fact, one of my affirming statements is, "I am my own teacher", as I believe I am teaching myself about my strengths and blessings. When I first wrote my list of affirmations, there were ten statements. Slowly, as my confidence grew, the list went up to twenty-five statements. The list now has between 100 and 150 statements that I know by heart. Please do not confuse this with being big-headed or arrogant. As I have discussed in Chapter 3, knowing your strengths is essential, whether you are a child or an adult.

An example of how affirmations can be a state changer

I was going into a school one morning, when I started to feel quite agitated. I had no obvious reason for this, which only added to the uneasy feeling I had. The whole situation was strange. I wasn't panicking as such, but just felt very out-of-sorts. I was due to meet with a parent in the school, and as I was twenty minutes early, I took the time to set up the room we were to meet in. I sat for a moment, the uneasy feeling not shifting, and decided to write out my affirming statements. As I wrote the statements, I stopped and connected to the statements I thought were most pertinent to this situation. I wasn't just writing a list; I was 'feeling' the statements. So, when I wrote 'I am limitless', I pictured it and I felt it. It took me around five minutes to write and 'feel' my list, and I surprised myself by how different I felt when I had finished. I felt calm, empowered and back on an even keel again. Whatever the uneasy feeling was, it did not return that day, and I didn't waste any more time wondering why it appeared or what it was. The affirmations had helped me shift my state so I could move on with my day.

Imagery and visualisation create pictures in our mind that, if seen often enough, condition us to expect certain outcomes. The 'feeling' element of affirmations is reliant on us picturing ourselves living within an affirmation. So, if the affirmation is, "I am free to achieve all I want to", really picture how this feels, as if it is already happening. We can waste hours imagining bad things that haven't happened, so why not make better use of our imagination and help ourselves feel good rather than fearful, worried and/or anxious?

People see communication as something we do with other people, and of course this is true. But we also communicate with ourselves through our thoughts, beliefs and internal conversations. Creating and maintaining a Book of Positivity, developing an 'attitude of gratitude' and using affirmations help you to take positive control of your internal conversations. You will be using Transformative Communication with yourself to create a stronger internal narrative.

Motion affects emotion

Tony Robbins is an author and self-improvement life coach who has worked with thousands of people across the world. You will find a lot of his material on YouTube. Tony talks about the way in which we carry ourselves having a profound impact on our moods. When you are fed up, negative and lacking motivation, look at your body language. It is likely that you will be holding yourself in such a way that tells your brain, *This isn't going to be a good day*. Your brain duly obliges by releasing hormones and chemicals into your system that increase your stress and lower your mood further. A vicious cycle is in operation as your body language then gets even worse. Tony encourages us to notice when we are in a bad place and use our physiology to change our state. This can be done in the following ways:

- **Changing your breathing from shallow and quick to deep and slow.** I love what Tony says about smokers: "All smoking is, is taking a deep inhale and then releasing it slowly." Imagine doing that without inhaling toxins into your body!
- **Put your chest out and shoulders back.** A simple one, but very effective. Tony talks about what I call the 'Superman pose'. You may laugh, but standing like that and taking in deep and slow breaths for a minute or two can transform your mood. It is hard to be down when you hold yourself like Superman! Even if this only serves to make you laugh, at least it has elevated your mood. Be careful where you do this, or you might attract some very strange looks!
- **Walking with purpose.** I have tried this a few times when I have felt tired in a school. School corridors are often long, so give me the perfect opportunity to walk with purpose. Moving our bodies positively tells our brains, *We are ready for action; let's get to it!* If you struggle for motivation to do this, imagine you are walking towards someone or something you are really excited about.
- **Exercising.** It is well known that exercise releases endorphins in our brain that elevate our mood. You do not have to be bench-pressing 100 kg or running a marathon to change your state. Depending on where you are, fast walking, press-ups, sitting on a chair then getting up on repeat, a jog and/or bringing your knees to your hands are all ways of raising your heart rate and changing your state.

Quick tips to change state

There are many daily disciplines that can transform your thinking and feeling, improve your beliefs and elevate your physiology. Maybe in a follow-up book I can cover them all! For now, here are some tips that can act as additional positive state changers:

Pro-pro lists
The idea of a 'pros and cons' list to help with a dilemma is as old as time. How about trying a 'pros and pros' list? List all of the best outcomes for each potential decision you can make in a dilemma. This way you are making a decision based on positives, not negatives.

Identify the opportunity in every challenge
Every challenge represents an opportunity to develop and grow in some way. However, we are programmed from our childhood by messages we receive from our families, the media and societal negativity bias that lead us to complain, blame and be generally negative in the face of a 'problem'. However, every such 'problem' can be considered as coming with an opportunity, as shown in the following list. As such, the 'problem' could be viewed as:

- a chance to develop a skill we otherwise would not have had to use;
- a time when we use a skill that we may not have realised we had;
- a chance to develop a relationship;
- an opportunity to appreciate the way things are 'normally';
- a way by which we know what we can do 'next time'.

If we change our thinking sufficiently, we develop part of our internal narrative that says, *There are two types of experiences in life: positive experiences and opportunities for learning.*

Meditation and guided visualisations
Meditation often brings up images of a Buddhist monk sitting in a trance, but not all meditation is as intense as this. There are simple, short and relatively straightforward meditations and guided visualisations in their thousands on YouTube. Bedtime guided meditations, which are essentially stories for adults, can be particularly useful at the end of the day. Dr Joe Dispenza, author of *You Are the Placebo* (2014) and *Becoming Supernatural* (2017), discusses the benefits of meditation as being so far-reaching that they can impact on health, happiness, gratitude, relationships and overall well-being.

Summary

I know that using Superpower language and Empathic and Empowering language, alongside the other strategies I have suggested, will support you to help your child transform their internal narrative and Resilience. You have taken in a lot of information, and my wish for you is that what you have learnt has a transformative influence on you and your child(ren). I am also aware that you will have your own negative aspects of your internal narrative—everybody does. Practising some, if not all, of the tips suggested in this chapter can help you change your temporary state. Moreover, through doing these things consistently, you can be supported at a deeper level in developing a stronger internal narrative for yourself. You would then find that you are in a more sustainably positive state, freeing you up to put in place the Transformative Communication covered in the book. People often use 'lack of time' as an excuse for not practising some of the strategies suggested in this chapter. However, the Book of Positivity, and 'attitude of gratitude' in particular, are approaches that can be used when you only have a few minutes to spare. We often have small pockets of time when we might think, *I don't have long enough to do a job, but I've got a few minutes. I'll check Twitter!* While there is no problem with checking social media, a proactive approach would be to use those few minutes practising some of the daily disciplines that could make a significant, positive difference to you.

I am committed to self-development and have been lucky enough to come across books that have transformed my life. I always look for ways to share my learning and make it applicable to the people I work with. Through my reading and practices, I have found new ways of improving my thinking, uplifting my internal narrative, being more grateful, seeing the wonder in the world and becoming the best person I can be—a work in progress, by the way. I have taken ideas from many books and incorporated them as daily disciplines that have helped me write my own narrative and leave behind the damaging narrative that was once the backdrop to my everyday life. The ideas I have shared in this chapter have helped me and, subsequently, many people I have worked with. I very much hope they help you too.

Case study: The greatest transformation

To protect the anonymity of the person involved, there are elements of her story that are not appropriate to share. Suffice it to say that this young woman had one of the most challenging childhoods you can imagine. HM was a young single parent of two children. She lived in a small house with little or no support from family or friends. When I first visited HM, I wondered if she was at home, as all of the curtains were closed, and I waited at the door for what felt like an age. I had gone to do an assessment with HM regarding her daughter, with a view to giving HM advice about how to increase her daughter's confidence. It soon became apparent that HM was extremely wary of me. She was blunt and short in her responses and bordering on aggressive with her body language. At other times during my first visit, I could see that HM was defensive and vulnerable. I realised that for HM attack was the best form of defence. As I put my laptop away and just spoke to her about what I could offer, HM softened her body language and her self-doubt became abundantly clear. She told me about the plethora of professionals who had been to her door and how, from her point of view, rather than support her, they had only judged her—a perception driven by her toxic beliefs about herself. HM then struggled to engage with any of the professionals who had previously been involved.

At the start of our second session I noticed a handwritten list on A4 paper stuck to the wall in HM's lounge. The list read 'Routine … Play for ten minutes … Boundaries … Praise'. I asked, "What does all that mean?"

She curtly replied, "Some woman came and told me I have to play with [child's name] for ten minutes every day, get into a better routine and have boundaries and praise."

I then enquired, "Did the woman tell you how to do all of that?"

The short response of HM was, "Did she f*c*!" before adding, "They never do."

I soon established that the well-meaning lady who had tried to help HM had elaborated on how to best support her daughter, but HM's state was resigned and unmotivated. She felt judged and was thinking, *Here we go again*. Consequently, she had not taken in what the lady had said. There and then I decided that talking about strategies for HM's daughter would be pointless at that juncture. I wanted to support HM in changing her view of herself and change her state (thoughts, emotions, beliefs and physiology). Without this, all the advice about Transformative Communication to use with her daughter would have made no difference at all, as she would not have been in the frame of mind to apply it. I was determined not to be just another professional who didn't give HM what she needed.

I empathised with HM and told her that first and foremost I wanted to support her, and then further down the line we would look at strategies she could put in place with her daughter. HM cried as she told me she felt like she was failing as a parent, but her way was the only way she had ever known how to survive. Here, the nail had been hit on the head: HM had lived in survival mode for so long, that living any other way scared her. This is why she was aggressive and defensive and kept people at arm's length. As HM began to trust me, she opened up about her childhood and told me that she had an older child who was now in the custody of a family member. She had been through many traumatic times and couldn't see how remarkably well she was doing given the circumstances. As I do with lots of parents I work with, I recommended *Feel the Fear and Do It Anyway*. Within hours of the session, HM sent me a text with a picture of the book, with 'This the one you mean?' accompanying it. I smiled broadly, knowing she had started her transformation just by acting on the advice I had given her. From that moment, I felt so invested in supporting HM, primarily because she needed the support, but also because I knew she genuinely wanted to make positive changes despite having every reasonable excuse not to try.

HM's internal narrative was toxic. She doubted herself at every turn. Often she would say, "I understand what you mean, but I can't do that" in response to self-improvement strategies. 'I can't do that' wasn't just a stock phrase she used. HM genuinely felt this in every part of her. Nonetheless, HM was reading 'Feel the Fear', taking on board our conversations and starting to see that blaming and complaining about the people who had mistreated her only served to continue to hand her power over to these people. HM was brilliantly responsive to my ideas. I spoke about the myth that eating healthily is expensive and told her that a bag of frozen vegetables was 89p at our local supermarket. Hours later she sent me a picture of a receipt that included frozen vegetables, with 'You were right' written alongside it. I encouraged her to exercise when she told me she used to like running but thought the neighbours would make fun of her if she went out in running gear. We spoke about how to take ownership of thoughts and feelings and let others think what they choose to. The next time I visited, HM had been running and decided to join the gym, despite being extremely self-conscious.

After a small break because of a school holiday, I visited as planned, and for the first time since I had met HM, the curtains were open. She smiled as she greeted me and offered me a cup of tea—another first. As I walked through to the lounge, I was taken aback to see that she had completely redecorated, got new furniture and added a few features to the living area that transformed it from dark and foreboding to warm and homely. HM looked uncomfortable when I told her how amazing the lounge looked, and I highlighted the skills she had shown to achieve the transformation. She quickly dismissed her efforts, but I saw a pride in her body language, even if she was embarrassed. We spoke about her finding a part-time job. I saw that HM had so much to offer, that it seemed a waste for her to sit at home for most of every day. HM told me that she had a criminal record for a relatively minor misdemeanour when she was very young, and this had always put her off looking for a job. We discussed this and did some problem-solving, but I was wary of pushing too hard with her, as I could see that disclosing her criminal record would make her feel shame, and I did not want her to regress into negative cycles of thinking. To my delight, a few weeks later I attended a meeting at school, and HM casually dropped into the conversation that she had been working in a new job for a few weeks.

When I met this young woman, who had suffered terrible trauma in her life, she was snarling, defensive, resentful and isolated. She sat in the dark all day in her undecorated lounge. She had no energy and was racked with self-doubt. Now she was employed, she went to the gym regularly, her home was warm and welcoming and she saw herself as being worthy of care and love. Whenever I talk about HM, I feel a sense of glowing pride. She is the epitome of someone who had such a negative internal narrative, that she was locked in multiple vicious cycles. She still has self-doubt and dismisses her achievements—twenty-eight years of negatives takes an awful lot of undoing. However, seeing HM's incredible progress resulted in one of the most satisfying feelings I have had in my career. I advised HM to practise many of the tips I have shared with you in this chapter. Heeding this advice (that she had been hugely sceptical of), along with her indomitable spirit, led her to take small steps that have seen her transform herself into a wonderful role model to her children.

Everybody deserves a chance to be happy. In all cases, the person who can make that happen is staring back at them in the mirror.

Final summary

Throughout the pages of this book I hope you have taken ideas of how, using Transformative Communication, you can transform your child's internal narrative (inner voice), leading to increased levels of Resilience and, in turn, more desirable behaviour. The internal narrative refers to the perceptions a child has about themselves and the world around them—the 'story' they tell themselves about their life, without knowing they are in that process. Rarely, if ever, will anyone have a perfect internal narrative (remember negativity bias?), but by regularly using Transformative Communication (Superpower language and Empathic and Empowering responses), you will teach your child positive Resilience—much more empowering than the typical survival Resilience I refer to in Chapters 1 and 4. Subsequently, you are likely to see your child transform their ability to:

- overcome setbacks;
- learn from setbacks;

- resolve conflicts;
- take responsibility for their behaviour;
- go out of their comfort zone to try things they doubt their ability in and/or feel uncomfortable doing.

All of the above are indicators of increased positive Resilience and replace the less desirable survival behaviours I detailed in Chapter 1.

Children spend much of their time being expected to meet ideals set by other people—mainly adults, but also siblings, peers, the media, television, films, social media and the world around them in general. Typically, when children meet ideals, they are given general praise, and they feel a brief sense of pride, happiness and even relief. In the current world we live in, when a child does not meet the ideals set by other people, they perceive that they are criticised, corrected, dismissed, ignored and/or rescued. So, whether a child meets external ideals or not, they learn very little about the positive strengths they have to impact on everyday situations. Superpower language helps children become aware of their unique strengths, and by using Superpower language in context, you will be giving your child(ren) concrete examples of how they show such strengths, so their Superpowers become part of who they see themselves as being.

The use, in particular, of Empathic and Empowering language helps parents look beyond the behaviour of their child to what that behaviour is translating—remember, a child's behaviour is a direct translation of their internal narrative (inner voice).

For parents, some obvious benefits of using Empathic and Empowering language are: your child comes out of crisis quicker, survival behaviours occur less often and your child is more compliant. While we would most probably all like our child(ren) to behave appropriately, the results from using Empathic and Empowering language are more far-reaching and can have a transformational impact on the child–parent relationship. I have experienced parents who have told me that their previously averse-to-physical-contact child has 'suddenly' become more tactile and loving. Other parents have said that, having applied Empathic and Empowering language regularly, they find it so much easier to like and understand their child. Some parents have indicated that their change in approach has made them realise that they have been carrying resentment from their own childhood into their parenting style, and Empathic and Empowering language has helped them understand how they would have felt as a child.

Additionally, and crucially, by recognising how your child is feeling, the problem they are experiencing and/or what their inner voice is telling them, you are helping your child understand themselves better—this is a great gift to present your child with. When you add empowering language that tells your child of the unique strengths they have to transform a seemingly negative scenario, this gift becomes transformative to your child's internal narrative.

Imagine for a moment—even as an adult—truly believing:

I am adaptable to any situation.

I have the ability to solve most of the problems I face.

My skills are greater than the challenges I encounter.

A child is constantly open to new learning, and the messages we give a child have a significant impact on what they learn about themself and the world around them. A child's internal narrative can be guided by toxic beliefs developed automatically over a period of time without question or challenge. By using Transformative Communication, we are supporting children to develop an internal narrative guided by understanding, empathy and Superpowers. It is this internal narrative that will govern a child's Resilience and has a telling role, then, in how that child develops and behaves as they mature.

Your child can become anyone they wish to be. In the end—IT'S ALL NARRATIVE.